D1162188

RELIGIOUS LIBERTY:

AN END AND A BEGINNING

Religious Liberty:
An End and a Beginning

THE DECLARATION ON RELIGIOUS
FREEDOM: AN ECUMENICAL DISCUSSION

Edited by JOHN COURTNEY MURRAY, S.J.

The Macmillan Company, New York

Collier-Macmillan Ltd., London

Library of Congress Catalog Card Number: 66-24891

FIRST PRINTING

The translation of the Declaration on Religious Freedom is taken from *The Documents of Vatican II*, published by Guild Press, America Press, and Association Press, and copyrighted 1966 by The America Press. Used by permission.
We wish to thank the Ampleforth Abbey and College, England, for permission to reprint "The Freedom of the Christian" by John L. McKenzie, S.J., which appeared in the June 1966 issue of *The Ampleforth Journal*.

The Macmillan Company, New York
Collier-Macmillan Canada Ltd., Toronto, Ontario

Printed in the United States of America

Contents

Preface

In one of his discourses to the conciliar fathers toward the conclusion of the Council, Pope Paul VI spoke this sentence: "The discussion is coming to an end; understanding is to begin." The statement is programmatic. Lengthy and laborious discussion went into the composition of the conciliar text. In the end, probably no one was fully satisfied with any of them, as might have been expected, given the size of the great assembly that met for four years, and given too the diversity of competence and preoccupation among its international membership. In any event, the texts —all sixteen of them—made a host of affirmations, to which there was very little final dissent. Many of them were touched with novelty. All of them were inspired by the will to make the tradition of the Church more explicit in her manner of statement, and more intelligible and relevant to the present moment in history.

An affirmation, however, is one thing; the understanding of the affirmation is a further matter. All the texts are now in the public domain, subject to study, open to an effort at understanding by all who may be interested, whether Catholic or non-Catholic. And it is to be expected that the process of understanding will be informed by the critical sense that respect for the truth always requires.

The Institute on Religious Freedom, organized by the Bellarmine School of Theology of Loyola University, which was held in North Aurora, Illinois, on February 25-26, 1966, marked a significant moment in the quest for understanding of the document that Pope Paul VI called "one of the major texts" of the Council—the Declaration on Religious Freedom. Nine discourses were given, each followed by discussion, both formal and informal. They are published in this volume, in order to assist, one hopes, still further discussion and thus to advance the process of understanding.

My own paper deals with one aspect of the three-year-long conciliar argument that resulted in the final declaration. From the beginning there was no doubt that the vast majority of the conciliar fathers were resolved to affirm the human right to religious freedom. The problem was to make the case for the affirmation. It was not surprising that this problem arose. Nor is it surprising that it still exists. Argument about the reasons for religious freedom has been one of the great themes of serious conversation through many centuries, even among those who affirm with conviction their belief in religious freedom. Hence the conciliar moment in the argument may be of general interest.

Dr. Jerald C. Brauer, dean of the School of Theology,

University of Chicago, takes up the same theme with the mind of the historian. Men of the past have made arguments for religious freedom out of the tradition of the "rights of Englishmen" in the sense of the British Constitution, or out of the tradition of the "rights of man" in the sense of the Enlightenment. What is the argument today? Interestingly—and validly, one must think—he sees the root of the argument in the "convergence" of many philosophies on the idea of the "self" and its dignity.

Fr. Francis J. Canavan, S.J., associate editor of *America,* looks at the declaration from the standpoint of the political scientist. With critical eye, he sees its argument deficient— as indeed it is—through a failure to fully appreciate the political dimension of the issue. Invocation of the ancient political "principal of consent" would have strengthened it at one point, and at another, full use of the juridical principal of "equality before the law."

The problem of the precise relation between religious freedom, in today's technical sense, and the doctrine of the Scriptures was much argued at the Council. Dr. David Noel Freedman, professor at the San Francisco Theological Seminary, examines the problem as an Old Testament scholar. Rightly, he misses reference to the Old Testament in the declaration. One version of the text had contained a brief paragraph on God's education of the people of the Old Testament in freedom and for freedom. But it was omitted in the end—perhaps unfortunately.

Dr. Freedman offers much important historical material for study, notably with a view to understand how slow a growth freedom is. Fr. John L. McKenzie, S.J., of the University of Chicago and Loyola University, deals with the New Testament. Regrettably, he does not speak of the

precise issue raised by the declaration, and raised too by
much ecumenical literature—whether it is enough to say
that religious freedom is simply "in harmony with Scripture," or is "rooted in Scripture," or whether one ought
to say that it is an "exigence" of scriptural doctrine. The
issue is subtle, but real. He does note the next question,
unavoidable—even if anyone cared to avoid it—after the
declaration, namely, the question of Christian freedom. On
this complicated question he puts forward some highly
personal views.

There is a saying that one never knows what one has
said until one finds out what others have heard, especially
when the others stand outside the context of the speaker's
presupposition. From this valid point of view, the next two
essays are of particular importance and value. Dr. Victor
G. Rosenblum, director of the program in law and social
science at Northwestern University, has the lawyer's attitude. He estimates the declaration to have the measure of
vagueness necessary and desirable in a constitutional document. The question is: what are the "legal requirements"
that follow from its principles? The question is legitimate,
and not easily answered. It is a theme necessary of further
discussion.

Dr. Philip S. Denenfeld, professor of English at Western
Michigan University, views the declaration in the particular perspective of the doctrine of the American Civil
Liberties Union, in which he has long been active. The
issue is the relation between the declaration and the First
Amendment. He notes agreements, but more significant
differences. And thus he launches another theme of discussion, a topic into which the declaration did not formally
enter: what are the implications of the declaration for a
larger theory of church-state relationships? And is the

doctrine of the ACLU on church and state, especially in what concerns education, to be the object of some univocal agreement? These are good questions.

With wonted wit and urbanity, Dr. J. V. Langmead Casserley, of Seabury-Western Theology Seminary, returns the question to a historical-theological state. All the modern liberties were indeed liberations from religio-political forms of repressions. Today, however, the tables have turned. It is not irreligion but religion that seeks freedom of expression. Once religious freedom was the child of skepticism. Now it is the child of faith. This faith, however, which acknowledges the value of an "agnosticism of definition" with regard to God, is indeed in the Christian tradition, but was lost from view amid the flickering lights of the Enlightenment. The Christian faith of today is faithful to itself in its affirmation of the freedom of faith.

Finally, Fr. George Van Massenhove, S.J., a visitor to our shores from Belgium, comments with the wisdom of simplicity on the facts of contemporary society—pluralist, secular, personalist in its ideals—in their relation to the conscience of the man who wills to affirm his adherence both to the certainties of Christian faith and to the ideal of societal freedom.

I am grateful to the Bellarmine School of Theology, which organized the institute—especially to William C. Cunningham, S.J., and John J. Kilgallen, S.J., its able coordinators, and to Thomas M. Gannon, S.J., for extensive editorial assistance in preparing these papers for publication. It is my hope that this volume may command the interest of those who wish to argue the issue of religious freedom in some depth.

JOHN COURTNEY MURRAY, S.J.

Woodstock, Maryland

PART I

THE DEVELOPMENT OF THE CONCILIAR DOCUMENT

The Declaration on Religious Freedom: A Moment in Its Legislative History

JOHN COURTNEY MURRAY, S.J.

THE first schema (or draft-text) on religious freedom was presented to the conciliar fathers on November 19, 1963, as chapter five of the schema on ecumenism. It was not subjected to formal discussion in the aula. However, in the course of the debate on ecumenism many comments were made on it, and many more were later sent in writing to the Secretariat for the Promotion of Christian Unity. The text was therefore revised at a meeting of the secretariat in February-March 1964. Changes of considerable importance were made, but the doctrinal line of the second schema remained substantially the same as that of the first schema (let them be so identified). The second schema was fully discussed in the aula on September 23-25, 1964. It then was so thoroughly revised that, in presenting the third text to the fathers on November 17, 1964, the "relator" was obliged to say that it "differs greatly from the text which was discussed in the aula." A new doctrinal line, as well as a new structure, had been adopted by the secretariat. This doctrinal line remained substantially the same through the subsequent three revisions. It is the line of the definitive declaration, promulgated on December 7, 1965.

The purpose of this essay is to set forth briefly and to compare the two doctrinal lines that appeared respectively in the first two schemata and in the third and subsequent ones. The essay, therefore, is a study of only one moment in the legislative history of the declaration. But this aspect has a certain centrality.

I

It is fair to characterize the first schema as a declaration of a theory of "freedom of conscience." The formula itself appears twice, and it is elsewhere implicit. The formula, "religious freedom," is used eight times as the equivalent of "freedom of conscience." The theme of "conscience" runs all through the text.

The problematic interpretation of religious freedom, as conceived in the first schema, was decisively influenced by the fact that the issue was taken up within the context of ecumenism. It was therefore stated in the *Relatio* (the presentation of the schema to the conciliar fathers) that "the first pastoral problem" to be considered was this: "How are Catholics, in virtue of their faith, to conduct themselves in their relations with those who do not adhere to the Catholic faith?" Properly speaking, this is a moral, not a juridical, problem. It does not immediately raise an issue of human rights as such; rather, the question concerns the moral virtues to be practiced in interpersonal relationships between Catholics and non-Catholics. Thereafter, the schema goes on to consider the juridical problem, that is, the question of freedom of conscience as a principle governing the relations among citizens as such, within organized civil society, and under the legitimate rule of government.

These two problems are evidently distinct and different, quite as different as the relationships in question—in the one case, ecumenical and dialogic, and in the other case, political and legal.

The schema bases its answer to the moral-ecumenical problem on the Catholic doctrine of the freedom of the act of Christian faith. It follows from this doctrine that Catholics are never to bring coercion to bear upon others not of their faith. In this sense, as the *Relatio* explains, "the disciples of Christ are not permitted to infringe the religious freedom of the individual person." This religious freedom is an immunity from coercion in what concerns man's personal relations with God. But this "negative" aspect of religious freedom is completed by a "positive" aspect. The *Relatio* continues: "On the contrary, they (the disciples of Christ) are to respect and esteem the right and duty of non-Catholics to follow the dictates of their own conscience, even when, after serious and adequate investigation, it errs in good faith." Religious freedom is freedom of conscience, and freedom of conscience is to be positively defined as "the right of the person to the free exercise of religion according to the dictates of conscience." The object or content of this right is not simply negative—an immunity, a "freedom from" coercion; it is also positive—a "freedom for" action according to conscience.

The schema, and its explanation in the *Relatio*, establishes a necessary relation between the theological doctrine of the freedom of Christian faith and the notion of freedom of conscience in its positive aspect, as formally grounded on an ethical doctrine with regard to the role of conscience in the religious and moral life. Thus the schema: "The human person, endowed with the capacity for conscious and free action, can fulfill the will of God only inasmuch as the divine law is apprehended through the mediation of the dictates of conscience. Hence the person can attain his ultimate end only by forming judgments of conscience and by faithfully following their dictates. Hence the man who sincerely obeys his conscience has the intention of obeying God Himself. And he is worthy of respect." This argument is further developed with a view to showing the irreplaceability of the personal conscience in the religious life. This completes the doctrine of the schema with regard to the moral-ecumenical problem.

Then the schema, in the words of the *Relatio*, "takes a further step," to the juridical problem of freedom of conscience in the social and civil order. The schema states its thesis: "The Holy Synod solemnly affirms that in religious matters, provided the common good is not impaired, the right to freedom of conscience in its external exercise is always and everywhere valid and is to be recognized by everyone." Or, in the words of the *Relatio*, ". . . all men and every man who in religious matters follows his conscience has a natural right to true and authentic religious freedom." This right is valid "for every human person, whether in the matter of faith his conscience be right and true or right and erroneous, provided that he sincerely follows the dictates of conscience." The passage to the juridical order is made by this statement: "This personal freedom (of conscience) is not really or effectively recognized, if it cannot express itself in external and public activity. For this reason, no one is to be deprived of the external exercise of his freedom (of conscience) in the human community and in civil society" (except for certain reasons—a matter that does not concern us at the moment.)

From this premise the schema proceeds to a strong condemnation of all forms of religious persecution and discrimination by governments. Their evil lies in the violation of "the rights of the Creator and Saviour of man and of the sacred rights of the human conscience and of the family or peoples." The positive duty of government is thus briefly stated: "Human powers ought to pay heed to justice and equity towards all who in matters religious obey the dictates of their conscience." Always the argument returns to conscience and its dictates.

In these terms the schema makes its case for freedom of conscience, both in its positive and in its negative aspect, as a civil right, valid against all social forces and against government itself. They are the same terms in which the case is made for freedom of conscience as a principle governing ecumenical relationships among Christians. In brief, the terms are a theory of the rights of the sincere conscience—the conscience of the man who sincerely desires to follow the will of God, even though he may be mistaken in his understanding of the will of God. The foundation of the right to the free exercise of religion, privately and publicly, is the sincere conscience and its dictates. The object or content of the right is both negative and positive, in the sense explained.

The second schema, which appeared as an appendix to the schema on ecumenism, continued to view the issue within the perspectives set by a primary preoccupation with the issue of ecumenical relationships. And it followed substantially the same doctrinal line as the first schema. For the rest, it exhibited two characteristics worthy of note for the present purpose.

First, the ethical doctrine of conscience is reinforced by the introduction of a new idea—the divine call of man to salvation in the full Christian sense, that is, a share in the divine nature. As the *Relatio* explains: "This divine call, which constitutes the highest dignity of the human person, is the nerve, as it were, by which the whole argumentation is pervaded and strengthened." It is "the foundation of the argument." Although the formula, "freedom of conscience," no longer appears, the theory itself remains. The *Relatio* thus paraphrases the text: "The foundation of these rights (in matters religious) consists in the strict obligation to respect human dignity or to observe the law of God as it is apprehended by the sincerely formed conscience. All this induces in others an obligation not to put obstacles in the way of the free following of the call of God. The freedom within human society and community to follow one's own conscience in religious matters is the highest good proper to every person, and it is, in consequence, a true and strict personal right." The right still finds its foundation in the obligation to follow the dictates of conscience.

The second characteristic is already visible in the first. The notion of human dignity and of religious freedom as "the right of the person" (the phrase occurs four times) has begun to move into central focus. This theme affords the first thread of continuity between the second schema and the third. However, the dignity of man is formally identified with his free fidelity to the imperatives of the conscience that is rightly, that is, sincerely, formed. From freedom of conscience, in this sense, there is drawn, as an inference, the juridical conclusion that there exists a right to the free exercise of religion in society: "Men are made in the image of God and are called to a participation in the divine nature. It is their honor that they should obey the will of their Creator and Saviour according to the dictates of conscience. From this source there arises the right to religious freedom in society, in virtue of which men are entitled to practice their religion privately and publicly, and are not to be hindered from its practice by any manner of coercion." The object or content of the right is still conceived, as in the first schema, both positively and negatively.

A further comment is necessary. The first and the second schema move entirely on the plane of theological and ethical argument. They make no attempt to present the subject in historical perspective. They seem to be stating "eternal truths." There is no evidence of historical consciousness, that is, an awareness of the developments that have occurred in the secular world and in the thought of the Church.

It is not possible here to analyze the conciliar discussions of the first two texts. It must be sufficient, first, to note that the discussion was extremely confused, and second, to identify the main source of the confusion.

The fact was that a contention arose between two positions, neither of which clearly defined the state of question, or fully articulated itself, under due regard for all necessary distinctions. The schema asserted that the man of sincere conscience, even though he be in error, has the right to religious freedom, meaning to the public profession, practice, and observance of his religion, and to its public teaching, according to the dictates of his own conscience. The foundation of his right is his own conscience and its sincerity; the content of the right is two-fold—positively, the free exercise of his religion, and negatively, immunity from coercive constraints or restraints. This position was opposed by another, which asserted that the man who is in error, even though he be sincere, has no right to religious freedom, no right to the public manifestation of his error, whether in action or, more particularly, in public teaching. The reason for this counterassertion was that rights must be founded on the objective order of truth, not on the subjective dictates of conscience. Furthermore, it is illegitimate to make an inference from the subjective order of conscience to the objective order of rights.

Both of these positions are simplistic. When they clashed, the inevitable result was confusion. It may be worthwhile to sort out the confusions.

One view rightly insisted, as a matter of moral principle, that man is bound to conform his belief and action to the objective truth. It also rightly insisted, as a matter of moral-juridical principle, that all rights must be founded on what is objectively true. But this manner of objectivism, so baldly stated, will hardly do. It overlooks the principle that objective truth becomes a norm of action only in the internal forum of conscience, as conscience itself apprehends the truth and its imperative character. It also overlooks the further truth that the laws of conscience are themselves elements of the objective moral order. The principle, "Everyone is bound to follow conscience," is not simply a dictate of conscience; it is an imperative of the objective moral order, which therefore sustains the morality of action that proceeds from the right but erroneous conscience. Furthermore, there was a failure to realize that, if, as a matter of moral principle, a man has the duty to follow his conscience, he must also somehow have, as a matter of moral-juridical principle, the right to do his duty, that is, to follow his conscience.

The proximate source of the duty is indeed the subjective imperative of conscience, but the ultimate source is the objective moral principle that conscience must be followed. In parallel fashion, the proximate source of the right is the subjective imperative of conscience, which imposes the duty, but the ultimate source is the objective moral-juridical principle that a man has the right to do his duty. The moral-juridical principle is inseparable from the moral principle, as the juridical order is inseparable from the moral order. If, therefore, the duty to follow conscience has its ultimate foundation in the objective order of truth, so too has the right to follow conscience.

It may seem that the doctrinal line of the first and second schemata could rescue itself from objection by invoking the line of argument just stated. However, the rescue is not so easily effected, if one carefully examines the nature of the juridical order. This order, which is the order of rights, has to do with intersubjective relations among men. Within it, a man does not face—looking upward—the objective order of truth and morality. He faces—looking outward—"the others," who also have their duties and rights. No one may ever urge "rights" against the truth; the very notion is nonsensical. Rights are urged against the others. And when validly urged, they induce in the others an obligation to render what is due, to perform the action called for, or to omit an action for whose omission the claim is made. The others are obliged to acknowledge my claim; they may not reject it; and they can have no grounds on which to make a counterclaim that would invalidate my claim.

There is no difficulty, of course, in the case of the man of both right and true conscience. What his conscience dictates him to do is in accord with the objective order of truth. He has the duty to do it; he has the right to do it; the others have the duty to recognize the rightfulness of his claim to act; and they have no grounds on which to deny it, precisely because the action in question is in accord with objective truth. No man of good sense could dissent from this position. The difficulty concerns the man whose conscience is right but erroneous. He has indeed the duty to act in accord with his conscience, even though the action (or omission) is in violation of the objective order of truth and morality. This is a matter of moral principle. The question is whether he also has the right to do his duty, that is, whether the moral-juridical principle is also valid in his case. This issue is in dispute.

There are those who affirm the validity of the principle also in this case. Their argument is the one already outlined—that the right to do one's duty is founded ultimately in the objective moral order. There are, however, those who do not grant that the erroneous conscience may have rights. And their argument is not negligible. It proceeds from the nature of the juridical relationship. To the moral claim made by the one who asserts a right there must correspond a moral obligation to the one on whom the claim is made—the obligation to acknowledge the validity of the claim and to fulfill it. In this case, the agent asserts his duty to act according to his conscience, even though, in fact, his action is at variance with the objective moral order. But are others to take upon themselves a duty correspondent to his alleged right? It would seem not. Despite his error of conscience, the agent has indeed the duty to act according to his conscience; his sincerity guarantees for him the rightness of what he does. But the others? Another's error of conscience can create no duties in me, nor can it guarantee for me the rightness of his action. All my duties must have their foundation in the objective moral order, and, in this case, this foundation is lacking. There is, in fact, a foundation on which I can make a counterclaim. In the name of the moral order, I can deny the rightfulness of his claim and absolve myself of all duties with respect to it. Consequently, the moral-juridical principle that a man has the right to do his duty is not valid in the case of the sincere but erroneous conscience. This kind of conscience cannot call into being a true juridical relationship. So runs the argument.

The dispute here is the same one that arose over the interpretation of the statement in "Pacem in Terris": "This also is to be numbered among the rights of man, that he should be able to worship God according to the right norm of his own conscience and to profess his religion privately and publicly." In one view, this right exists only in the case of the right and true conscience; in the other view, its existence attaches to the right conscience, whether true or erroneous.

This, in brief, was the major objection encountered by the first two conciliar texts. It encountered an unresolved dispute within the Church with regard to the "rights of conscience." There was no clear tradition on the issue. In fact, the history of the doctrine of conscience as the source of duties and rights has been marked by controversy, from the days of Aquinas through the days of Suárez to the present time. It is altogether possible that the dispute outlined above may be resolved. The fact is that it has not yet been resolved. The doctrinal line of the first two texts took the liberal side in the dispute. But in the absence of a consensus, this line could not be made the basis of a conciliar statement.

There was the further difficulty that the phrase, "freedom of conscience," is laden with historical connotations. It came into currency in the post-Reformation era, when it carried overtones of "private judgment" in some Protestant sense. Even more serious, the phrase was part of the vocabulary of nineteenth-century Continental laicism, which connoted the reactionalist dogma of the "lawless conscience," absolutely autonomous in its individual judgments, not subject to a transcendental order of truth. Hence the phrase is suspect in Catholic circles, as the conciliar debates clearly proved. It has no standing as the symbol of an acceptable doctrine that could furnish the foundation of a sound doctrine on religious freedom in its juridical sense. Efforts have been made to endow the phrase with a true sense and with a valid standing—to transform the phrase into the symbol for the rightful freedom of man as a moral subject. Symbols, however, are not easily manufactured or manipulated. The phrase, "freedom of conscience," has not yet won an undisputed place in the Catholic vocabulary.

II

It was clearly necessary for the third schema to strike off along a new doctrinal line. And it did so. First of all, the schema became an independent "declaration," no longer attached to the schema on ecumenism. It lost none of its ecumenical value, of course. But it was released from its previous formal preoccupation with ecumenical relationships. Traditional doctrine on conscience and its duties is quite adequate to inspire that respect and reverence for others not of one's own faith, which creates ecumenical climate. It is not at all necessary to raise the issue of the "rights of conscience." Ecumenical relationships are not of the juridical order but of the higher order of charity and love between persons.

The third schema therefore took up the issue of religious freedom as a formally juridical concept. Here it was on solid ground. The technical definition of religious freedom as an idea and as a legal institution has long been established in the literature of constitutionalism. The definition is commonly accepted, and it is not only technically correct from a juridical point of view but also unexceptionable from a moral point of view. Religious freedom is a freedom from coercion; it is an immunity; its content is negative. Historically, the First Amendment to the Constitution of the United States launched this conception. The freedoms of the First Amendment, including the "free exercise of religion," were understood to be certain specified immunities; moreover, they were essentially related to the concept of constitutional government, which is twofold in its import. First, the powers of government are limited by a higher order of human rights; and second, it is "to secure these rights (that) governments are instituted among men" (Declaration of Independence). The political or civil freedoms of the First Amendment, unlike later freedoms or rights of the socioeconomic order, were not claims on society and government for positive action, but assurances against positive coercive action by government and society. "Congress shall make no law," government shall take no coercive measures, that would prohibit or abridge the exercise of the inalienable rights with which "all men . . . are endowed by their Creator." Moreover, constitutional law itself, embodied in the First Amendment, forbids the use of such coercive measures by the citizenry, whether as individuals or as organized in associations.

Hence the object of religious freedom as a juridical conception is not the actualization of the positive values inherent in religious belief, profession, and practice. These values, as values, are juridically irrelevant, however great their religious, moral, and social significance. The object of the right is simply the assured absence of constraints and restraints on individuals and groups in their efforts to pursue freely the positive values of religion. The only matters that are juridically relevant are, first, the limits that may be reasonably set to the free exercise of religion and, second, the duty of government and of society not to transgress these limits. This is good juridical philosophy. It is of the nature of a juridical formula—in this case, religious freedom—simply to set outside limits to a sphere of human activity, and to guarantee this sphere against forcible intrusion from without, but not to penetrate into the interior of this sphere and to pronounce moral or theological judgments of value on the activity itself. Such judgments exceed the category of the juridical, which is concerned with interpersonal relationships. They likewise exceed the competence of the forces of juridical order—the forces of law and of political authority.

Therefore, in its juridical sense as a human right, religious freedom is a functional or instrumental concept. Precisely by reason of its negative content it serves to make possible and easy the practice of religious values in the life of men and of society. It serves to assure full scope for the manifold manifestations of freedom in religious matters. This too is the function of religious freedom as a legal institution embodying a civil right. It is to create and maintain a constitutional situation, and to that extent to favor and foster a social climate, within which the citizen and the religious community may pursue the higher ends of human existence without let or hindrance by other citizens, by social groups, or by government itself. These ends, and the actual pursuit of them, are of the metajuridical order. They are related to the inner dynamism of the human spirit as such, which is remote from direction or control by any forces of the juridical order.

This was the notion of religious freedom that was accepted in the third schema. It is worthwhile to note that it is poles apart from the notions of "freedom of conscience" and "freedom of cult" that were characteristic of nineteenth-century Continental laicism. However, to pursue this subject would carry the argument too deeply into history.

The third schema was also on solid ground when it defined religious freedom in terms of a twofold immunity. No one is to be restrained from acting according to his convictions. In the first place, the distinction reflects two stages of historical progress. The first immunity came to be commonly recognized in the post-Reformation era, as the iniquity of the territorial principle (*cuius regio eius et religio*) gradually forced itself upon the consciousness of men. But the recognition of the second immunity came more slowly. In fact, a group of fathers at Vatican Council II were still unwilling to recognize it as constituent of religious freedom. This aspect of the question is, in fact, the crucial aspect.

The first schema and the second had incorporated the distinction of the two immunities, but had failed to note its significance for the argument. The two texts seemed to suppose, for instance, that the argument from the freedom of Christian faith and the argument from the rights of conscience were somehow adequate to prove the immunity of the person both from coercive constraint and also from coercive restraint. This, however, is not true. From the necessary freedom of the act of Christian faith—or of any other kind of final religious commitment, even one of atheist tenor—it does indeed follow that no man may be constrained either to believe against his will or to act in a manner contrary to his own beliefs. The argument is obvious and also apodictic. But it is apodictic only because it is impossible to prove that any external authority exists that is rightfully empowered to constrain religious belief and action. On the other hand, the question of coercive restraint of action according to one's own convictions presents a different aspect, both historically and speculatively.

Historically, there have been governments that asserted, as their religious prerogative, the right to repress public manifestations of religious belief that were contrary to the tenets and practices of the legally established "religion of the state." At the same time, they claimed no right to force anyone to accept the "religion of the state" against his own will and belief. What is more important, there was at the Council itself strong representation of the school of Catholic thought that maintained, as a matter of principle, the right of the "Catholic state," so called, to repress the public activities—the worship and the propaganda—of those who act according to their conscience but in a manner at variance with the tenets and practices of Catholicism. Moreover, this school of thought maintained that such a right on the part of the "Catholic government" is entirely compatible with Catholic doctrine on the freedom of faith and on the rights of conscience.

Consequently, in order to prove that religious freedom includes immunity from restraints on action according to conscience, it is not sufficient to attend only to the theological and ethical aspects of the issue. The political aspect becomes decisive. It is necessary to confront the question, whether and under what conditions government has the right to restrain citizens from public action according to their own beliefs. In other words, is there some special feature of civil authority that empowers it to disregard and override the claim of the citizen to immunity from coercive interference when he acts in religious matters according to his conscience? Or in more general terms, what are the functions and the limits of the powers of government in what concerns religion?

The first schema was not satisfactory in its answer to this question. It asserted that "in public life the external exercise of freedom of conscience may not be hindered, unless it goes against the common good or the objective order of the rights of God, the Creator and Saviour, and of the inalienable rights and freedoms of the human person." This, however, was precisely the position of the partisans of the historic "Catholic state." Public worship and public propaganda of a heretical sort, they said, goes against the common good, offends the objective order of the rights of God, and violates the right of a Catholic people to undisturbed possession of its common faith. What is more, the principle stated by the first schema would be unintelligible in societies whose governments are professedly secular in their purposes, and it would be even more meaningless to governments controlled by irreligious ideologies. This defect was serious in a document that was to be directed to the whole world.

The second schema was hardly more satisfactory. It asserted that "the exercise (of human rights in religious matters) may not be limited except in so far as it seriously contravenes the purpose of society, which consists in the complex of those conditions of social life in which men can achieve their own perfection with greater fullness and facility, and can at the same time respect the inalienable rights given by God to men in common." The phrase, "common good," is dropped, but the notion itself returns in an implicit citation from "Mater et Magistra." Again, however, the criterion for governmental or legal limitation of the free exercise of religion is stated with such generality and lack of precision as to make it useless as a juridical norm. The schema again avoided the issue of the "Catholic state." And again it did not come to grips with the issue of other types of states. The exigencies of the "common good" or of the "purpose of society" could readily be conceived in so broad a fashion as to warrant unjust and intolerable restrictions of rightful freedom.

At that, a growing awareness of the political dimension of the issue of religious freedom began to appear in the second schema. And the premise for the solution of the present question is laid down: "On their part, those who are in charge of public affairs are bound effectively to protect the right of the person to freedom in religious matters and to promote it in suitable ways. The reason is that the state has as its proper function not only to recognize and respect the rights of the person but also facilitate their exercise and to preclude the putting of obstacles in the way of men who are exercising their rights." Thus, the text begins to incorporate the concept of constitutional government—what is called in the Continental vocabulary the "juridical state." This is the political doctrine that Pius XII began strongly to evolve and that John XXIII further elaborated—the doctrine that the powers of government are limited by a superior order of human rights and are primarily to be employed in the protection and vindication of these rights. The first schema had merely referred to this doctrine in a footnote. In the second schema, the footnote is taken up into the text.

Furthermore, the second schema goes far beyond the first by venturing this statement of political principle: "The civil powers have no direct capacity and competence to determine or regulate the relations of citizens with their Creator and Saviour. In consequence, they may not subordinate religious communities to the temporal purposes of the state." This effort to define, in principle, the limitations of government in the order of religion was to be the occasion of much conciliar debate. In the end, the issue proved to be too complicated. And the effort to deal adequately with it would have led the schema far beyond the relatively narrow issue of religious freedom.

The third schema, however, does sharpen the positive affirmation, already introduced into the second schema, that the care of religious freedom devolves upon government: "It is the chief function of all governments to protect the inviolable rights of man. Therefore government is effectively to assume, by just laws, the safeguard and the care of the religious freedom of all citizens. It is also to take care that the equality of all citizens before the law is not violated for religious reasons." This principle serves to clarify the issue of the norm that should control the action of law and government in restriction of the free exercise of religion. This norm cannot be either the common good or the purpose of society. Since religious freedom is declared to be a human right, the common good itself, and the purpose of society as well, require that the right to the free exercise of religion should be fully protected. Neither of these concepts can be alleged as a norm of restriction. A different and more narrowly defined juridical criterion is therefore needed. The schema finds it in the concept of "public order."

The concept is of frequent occurrence in the literature of constitutional law. Its content, however, is rarely defined with exactitude. The schema undertakes a definition.

First, public order is declared to be "that essential element of the common good which is committed to government in a particular way, in such wise the protection of it is to be accomplished by the coercive force of law." The underlying distinction here is between what is necessary for the sheer coexistence of citizens within conditions of elemental social order, and what is useful in promoting their collaboration toward more perfect conditions of social welfare and in insuring their fuller coparticipation in the benefits of social life. The category of the necessary is the category of public order. The wider category of the useful covers the more comprehensive concept of the common good. Furthermore, within the category of the socially necessary, the schema distinguishes three elements: the protection of the public peace against serious disturbance, the safeguard of public morality against serious violation, and the vindication of the common rights of all citizens against trespass. Unless public order in this triple sense is effectively insured, society ceases to be an order at all, and the very coexistence of men in society is endangered.

In these terms the schema lays down a sufficiently narrow criterion for legal or governmental restriction of the exercise of the right to religious freedom. The basic warrant of the restriction is "the right of society to protect itself against abuses which may be perpetrated on the specious title of religious freedom." This protection is to be furnished by government, "not in some arbitrary fashion, but in accordance with juridical norms." These norms are defined by the "exigencies of public order." And these exigencies are so stringent that they warrant the use of coercion in restriction of freedom. The basic reason is that, in the triple case, there is an issue of civil crime, and there is consequently the need for the application of penal laws in legitimate defense of fundamental social values.

The notion of public order—or more exactly, the phrase itself—awaked in some conciliar fathers the fear that it be the occasion of abuses by governments hostile to religion. If there is hostility, of course, such abuses can never be wholly precluded. However, the schema did the best it could to surround the notion with the necessary safeguards. First, public order was explicitly related to the common good; in consequence, the notion was given not only a juridical, but also a moral, content. Second, and more important, the third schema included, for the first time, a statement of the principle of the free society: "The freedom of man is to be respected as far as possible, and it is not to be restricted except in so far as necessary." This principle is rooted in the dignity of the human person. When it is recognized effectively, abuses of governmental power in the order of religion, as in other orders of social life, are likewise effectively barred.

In its first aspect, the doctrinal line of the third schema is a consistent structure of three parts. First, the contemporary juridical conception of religious freedom asserts the content of the right to be negative, an immunity from coercion. Second, to this notion of immunity there corresponds the constitutional concept of government as limited in its powers. In this case, these powers are limited by the human right to religious freedom, and they are also limited to the protection and vindication of this right. Third, this concept of limited government further yields a more narrow criterion for legal limitation of the free exercise of religion, namely, the necessary exigencies of the public order in its threefold sense. Inherent, therefore, in the notion of religious freedom is the notion of governmental incompetence in matters religious. This latter notion, however, has to be exactly understood. The constitutional provision for religious freedom is a self-denying ordinance on the part of government. That is to say, government denies to itself the competence to be a judge of religious belief and action. But this denial is not an assertion of indifference to the values of religion to man and to society. Nor is it a reassertion of the outworn laicist creed that "religion is a purely private matter." It is simply a recognition of the limited functions of the juridical order of society as the legal armature of human rights. Hence it is a recognition of the inviolability of the human person, individually and in association with others, in what concerns religious belief and action.

This brings up the second aspect of the doctrinal line adopted by the third schema. It has to do with the foundation of the right to religious freedom. The foundation of the right is no longer located in the "right conscience." Instead, the foundation is asserted to be "the dignity of the human person." Thus, the schema situates itself within the Catholic tradition; more exactly, it makes contact with the "growing edge" of the tradition. The schema explicitly adverts to the development of the political and juridical philosophy of the Church that has taken place in recent decades, as the menace of Continental laicism gave way to the more profound threat of "state-totalitarianism, the enemy of all human freedom, (which) has come to power in many regions of the world." The reflection of the Church, stimulated by new problems, has turned back upon aspects of the tradition that were neglected in the treatment of older problems. And recent popes have developed a doctrine by which "the human person is declared with increasing emphasis to be the foundation, the end, and the bearer of the whole of social life. Moreover, fuller light has been thrown on the truth that man, as a person, is the subject of rights which have their source in his very nature. This truth is valid in all areas of human life and activity, and particularly in matters of religious concern. Finally, the affirmation has been made with increasing clarity that the chief function of government is to protect, promote, and vindicate the natural rights of all citizens."

In consonance with the developed tradition of the Church on the political and juridical order, the third schema bases the right to religious freedom on the dignity of the human person. It can hardly be said that the schema develops the idea satisfactorily; it does no more than suggest the line of development to be followed. The argument would begin with the traditional truth that every man has the innate dignity of a moral subject. He is endowed with intelligence, with a capacity for self-awareness. He is therefore called to a consciousness of the sense of his own existence—its meaning and purpose as determined by a transcendent order of truth and moral values, which is not created by himself but is to be discovered by him in the total reality of existence itself. Man is also endowed with freedom, a capacity for love and choice. As a subject *sui juris*, he is called to realize the sense of his own existence through a life-long process of self-determination, motivated by his own personal judgments. Therefore, man is a responsible agent in a twofold sense: He is responsible for the conformity of his judgments of conscience with the imperatives of the transcendent order of truth, and he is responsible for the conformity of his external actions with the inner imperatives of conscience.

As a moral subject, man exhibits three characteristics. The first is personal autonomy. That is to say, in his necessary search for the sense of human existence, he is subject only to the laws that rule the order of truth—truth is so accepted only on pertinent evidence, the assent to truth is to be personal and free, the search itself is to be pursued in free communion with others. The second characteristic is the irreplaceability of personal judgment and choice in the moral life. Moral worth attaches only to a human act done deliberately and freely. The human subject cannot be endowed with moral worth from the outside, by the action of others that would attempt to substitute itself for the inner dynamisms of intelligence and freedom. The third characteristic is inviolability. Man's native condition as a moral subject, who confronts the demands of a transcendent order of truth and goodness, requires that he be surrounded by a zone or sphere of freedom within which he may take upon himself his ineluctable burden—that of responsibility for his own existence.

This human requirement for an environment of freedom is more stringent in what concerns man's relation with God. This relation is personal in that it is immediate, a relation of person to person. Therefore, it is to be freely entered, in response to the divine initiative. And in further consequence, the responsibility for the nature of the response, whether acceptance or rejection, is inexorably a personal responsibility, not to be shared with others or assumed by others, much less shifted onto others.

On all these counts it clearly appears that coercion brought to bear upon the human subject, especially in what concerns his relation with God, is not only a useless irrelevance but also a damaging intrusion. It does injury to man's personal autonomy. It stupidly seeks to replace what is irreplaceable. It does violence to the very texture of the human condition, which is a condition of personal responsibility. The conclusion is that an exigence for immunity from coercion is resident in the human person as such. It is an exigence of his dignity as a moral subject. This exigence is the source of the fundamental rights of the person—those politico-civil rights concerning the search for truth, artistic creation, scientific discovery, and the development of man's political views, moral convictions, and religious beliefs. In all these areas of human life, in which the values of the human spirit are directly at stake, the human person has the right to immunity from coercion—the right to the establishment and maintenance about himself of a zone of freedom, into which others are not permitted forcibly to intrude. This right is asserted against all "the others"—other individuals, others organized in social groups, and especially that impersonal "other" that is the state, the institutionalized agencies of law and government.

This argument may be stated more briefly. Inherent in the dignity of man as a moral subject is the exigence to act on his own initiative and on his own personal responsibility, especially in that vital area in which the sense of his own existence and his necessary pursuit of it, are at stake—that is to say, especially in matters religious. This exigence is a thing of the objective order; it is rooted in the given reality of man as man. Therefore, this exigence is permanent and ineradicable and altogether stringent. It is identically the basic imperative requirement that man should act in accordance with his nature. In the name of this objective exigence man asserts, in the juridical order and over all "the others," his right not be be hindered in acting according to his nature. He asserts his right to immunity from coercion, especially in matters religious. This is man's fundamental moral claim on others.

It is valid not only in its objective foundation, which is man's native dignity, but also in the crucial instance, in the citizen's confrontation with the authority that has charge of the juridical order. If there be an authority that might possibly enter a counterclaim to the claim of the human person to immunity from coercion in matters religious, this authority could only be government, which is responsible for the establishment and maintenance of the juridical order in society. However, the moral claim or right of the human person is original, as original as the human person itself, which is the foundation, the end, and the subject of the whole juridical order. The claims of government are only derivative, subordinate to the claims of the human person, and enlisted in support of these claims. Therefore, the basic exigence of the human person for immunity from coercion, and the human right that springs from it, are in possession. Government must accept the burden of proving that it has the right to bring coercion to bear. This, however, it cannot do, except when its own fundamental responsibility becomes controlling—in the case of a violation of public order; a contravention of the necessary conditions of social coexistence; a public offense that imperils the pillars of society, which are an order of equal justice for all citizens; the public peace which is the work of justice; and that minimum of realizable public morality whose maintenance is the just requirement of the citizenry.

This then is the doctrinal line that was installed in the third schema. It remained intact through the subsequent three revisions of the texts. The transition to it was a decisive moment in the legislative history of the text.

PART II

THE CASE FOR RELIGIOUS FREEDOM

Religious Freedom
as a Human Right

JERALD C. BRAUER

WHEN Vatican Council II, by an overwhelming vote, formally adopted the schema, Declaration on Religious Freedom, the entire world breathed a sigh of relief. No other document under discussion, including the declaration On the Relation of the Church to Non-Christian Religions with its section on the Jews, received so much attention from the secular world. All of mankind, including the Communist nations, were deeply interested in or at least curious about the debates that raged back and forth over this schema. To be sure, it was given particular attention in the American press and by the American people because of the special situation in this nation. It cannot be denied, however, that vast numbers of people, particularly intellectuals and the politicians in all of the Western nations and in many of the Eastern nations, followed the discussions and debates with more than usual interest. One need only recall the world-wide uproar occasioned by the events of the final two days of the third session in 1964. The hard fact is that countless numbers of people were convinced that the Roman Catholic Church, by definition, could not or would not pass a powerful statement concerning religious liberty. This strong document is eloquent testimony to the spirit of renewal embodied in Vatican Council II.

The schema on religious freedom must be seen in its total context. It is not an isolated document grudgingly presented to the modern world to convince it that the Roman Catholic Church had suddenly become open to the needs of modern man. It can be understood only as a genuine expression of the over-all intent of the Council to address itself with renewed vigor and purity to the fundamental questions of modern man. The Council, under the guidance of John XXIII's basic insight, correctly analyzed the central issue as that of modern man retaining his essential humanity in the midst of a highly developed technological society. The concern of the Council was to speak for the Church to the whole world, to all men, and not simply to the faithful. A profound effort was made through all the schemata to point to the uniqueness, the dignity, and the glorious possibilities of mankind as seen from the perspective of the Christian faith.

The schema on religious freedom was part of that effort; thus, it ought not to be judged in and of itself, but only in relation to the total work of the Council. It is interesting to note that the initial text was chapter five of the schema of the decree On Ecumenism. Intimate interrelationships between the declarations on ecumenism, religious freedom, and the relation of the Church to non-Christian

religions are evident to all who examine the documents.[1]
It is not only in the schema on religious freedom that statements on religious liberty are contained. References can
also be found in other schemata, particularly in the two
just mentioned, and especially, in the schema on the Pastoral Constitution on the Church in the Modern World.

If Vatican II marks a new epoch in the history of the
Roman Catholic Church as she enters the age of dialogue,
each of the schemata reflects this fact. Dialogue cannot be
carried on either between individuals or between groups
unless each side takes the other side seriously and assumes
that there is some truth in the other point of view. Dialogue is possible only when there is equal freedom for all
participants to be involved without undue advantage or
particular pressure. Genuine dialogue presupposes a condition of religious freedom whereby individuals and groups
actually possess the freedom to engage in exchange with
one another. There are at least six or seven references that
point to or imply religious freedom in the schema on non-
Christian religions.[2] This is particularly clear in the fifth
chapter, part of which reads, "The foundation is therefore removed for any theory or practice that leads to
discrimination between man and man or people and people,
insofar as their human dignity and their rights flowing
from it are concerned. The Church thus reproves as
foreign to the mind of Christ any discrimination against
men of harassment of them because of their race, color,
condition in life, or religion." [3] The schema on The
Church in the World of Today abounds with references
that either imply or distinctly state the necessity of religious freedom. Approximately thirty references could be

made to passages that collaborate with the insights and statements of the schema on religious freedom.[4]

Some of the references in the other schema refer to religious freedom as grounded in human nature itself apart from the insights of revelation. Other references are clearly grounded in the teaching and doctrine of the Christian faith. The limits of this paper demand that attention be paid only to the former, to religious freedom as a human right based only on insights other than religious or theological. The method of this paper will be first to engage in an analysis of religious freedom as a human right from the perspective of several philosophical traditions, and particularly, as seen in the historical context of its development. Secondly, an effort will be made to review the problem in light of more recent philosophical and psychological developments in the life of modern man.

The schema speaks of religious freedom as a human right, and in one place calls it an "inviolable right" of man.[5] Primarily, it handles the problem from the perspective of the human person demanding, by his very nature, religious freedom as an essential right. This places the schema, in some sense, in the tradition of the natural rights philosophy, which, being so basic to American experience, makes the document easily understood by the American mentality but easily open to a basic misinterpretation.

Religious freedom emerged late in Western culture. When it first appeared in the American context it developed not so much from the principles and activities of the traditional Christian churches, but primarily from philosophy of the Enlightenment and from the necessities of historic circumstances.[6] There must be a moment in history when the powerful presence of the idea coincides with the proper historical circumstances to create a moment of creative realization in human life, both personal and social. That is what happened for the first time in late eighteenth-century America.

Philosophically, religious freedom in America was grounded on the natural rights theory, which had had a long and checkered career from the Greek through Roman culture into Western society, until it received a fresh formulation in the seventeenth and eighteenth centuries. This has become so much a part of Western culture that it is doubtful that it will ever totally disappear, though it will undoubtedly be drastically modified from time to time. The natural rights theory involves a certain conception of nature, of man, and of the state built upon Enlightenment philosophy.

The Enlightenment followed a period of social and intellectual upheaval and embodied man's attempt to find a solid basis to replace the chaos left by religious wars and the uncertainty left by the creative breakthroughs in the scientific and philosophical realms. The discoveries in mathematics and physics pointed to the structure of nature and the world as an orderly process reflecting clearly formulated and unchanging laws. Immediate observation confronted one with a bewildering complexity of individual variations, but this was only apparent. Underneath and running through this appearance was a series of clearly defined universal principles or laws. These were a priori, not contingent on specific observation, and so provided a dependable or a calculable base that overcame all accidental or unusual factors and that prevented all excesses.

This view of nature provided the context for the natural rights theory.[7] Man was viewed as an integral part

of nature, indeed subordinated to it and, at the same time,
a reflection of it. That which was distinctive about man
was precisely that which was distinctive about nature.
Man, too, was a rational creature who embodied certain
universal principles or ideas. There was a continuity
between man and nature in their common participation in
universal laws. The true genius of man was not his uniqueness in nature or his transcendence at any point beyond
nature; rather, man's genius was that he embodied more
fully and articulated more consistently the fundamental
principles of the universe itself. That which made man an
individual, a reality of infinite worth, was not his individ-
uality or his particularity, but rather his most direct and
consistent reflection of the basic principles of nature itself.
In this way, Enlightenment philosophy could stress the
absolute importance of the individual human being, and
at the same time, ignore anything unusual or unique about
any given man.

If man was this kind of being, then he possessed as an
individual a set of special natural rights. They were natural
because they were grounded in the reality of the universe itself; they were dependent only upon nature. These
rights were present in every human being by virtue of his
being human; thus they were universal. They also had
content and norms. There was an oughtness and a give-
ness to them that could not be usurped by any power in
heaven or on earth. Not even God could countermand
these natural rights of man because the God of the
Enlightenment was the very nature of these principles.
For God to contradict or to cancel the rights would be
to contradict His own essence and His own nature. No

power on earth could rescind or control these rights because this would be a direct violation off the most fundamental principles of the entire universe.

It was quite clear that neither society nor the state had any power over natural rights. It is at this point that the "social contract" theory played such a prominent role in natural rights philosophy.[8] Neither society nor the state embodied the universal principles of nature in the same way as the human individual; thus, both society and the state were derivative from the individual. The theory held that man, in order to more fully realize his potential and to have sufficient security to do this, formed a social contract whereby certain rights and actions were surrendered by individuals and shared in a group or a society. This society, in turn, on behalf of individuals, created particular forms of the state with juridical power to carry through the wishes of society. Althusius sketched out this theory fully, but it received its first full embodiment during the American Revolution, both in the Declaration of Independence and in the American Constitution.[9]

The state was definitely required and played a very important role in the social contract theory, but it did not possess any sovereignty in itself, only a derivative sovereignty through the people. The state was to maintain peace and order, to promote the general welfare, and to provide the context in which man could flourish. It was to provide the positive laws and the necessary force to see that a constant effort was made in the direction of justice for each person in society, which was his due because of his nature as a man. Its basic goal was the temporal happiness of mankind. Althusius made an exact distinction between the human individual as a true person, and the state and all social organizations as only artificial persons. This made clear the fact that the state, and even society, was derived from the individual and not vice versa. All rights initially were found only in individual human beings. Part of these rights were voluntarily given up, first to society and then, through society, to the state. Natural rights, by definition, could not be given up by the individual. The list of rights varied somewhat, but there was a basic set affirmed by most Enlightenment philosophers. These rights were life, liberty, equality, and property. Among the natural rights in the category of liberty were religious liberty, freedom of speech, and freedom of assembly. The fullest codification of these rights is to be found in the Bill of Rights, or the first ten amendments to the American Constitution.

These rights were believed to be self-evident. The famous words of the Declaration of Independence state, "We hold these truths to be self-evident." That is, these rights are self-authenticating to the reason of mankind. One needs only to analyze nature and man with the instrument of reason, and he will immediately perceive the reality and the truth of these rights. They do not depend upon history, upon social circumstances, or upon the will of any earthly power. They are a part of the warp and woof of the universe, and they find their fullest and clearest expression in man. History is the story of the usurpation of these rights by dishonest political and religious leaders and institutions. So the *philosophes* argued, and maintained that natural rights could never be given up nor taken away from man except under duress or manipulation.

Why was religion listed as one of the natural rights of

man? There are both strong positive reasons and equally strong negative reasons for its inclusion. The Enlightenment was deeply interested in moral rectitude, or in the absolute certainty of moral principles. This was essential to its total point of view. Whatever difficulties religion presented, it was the guardian and the inculcator of the moral in the life of mankind and in society. Therefore, in a positive sense, religion was of the utmost importance to the Enlightenment mind. It was inconceivable to talk of inalienable rights and to ignore religion. This would over-look the very core of the Enlightenment's viewpoint. It is also interesting to note that, for men of the Enlightenment, universal principles, or the moral imperative, were upheld and extolled with a passion that was seldom encountered in any other facet of their activity.[10] The reality of the consistent, thoroughgoing, and universal moral law undergirded their thought. Even Newton's laws were thought to be a manifestation of this same divine law. By definition, reaction to and activity in response to this moral law had to be totally unfettered and fully free.

On the negative side, the *philosophes* were convinced that religious institutions and political tyrants were the two primary opponents to the natural rights of mankind. Their picture of history was a fall from innocence owing to the crafty manipulation of greedy, evil, power-hungry prelates and kings.[11] Unfortunately, they found ample evidence in their highly selective reading of history. If religion had proved to be one of the bulwarks of ignorance and superstition, then it had to be stripped of all powers of coercion and manipulation over mankind. Man had to be set free from the bondage of religious coercion in order to exercise his true humanity. Kant, in his famous treatise

on the Enlightenment, stated its theme when he called on
man to dare to use his understanding over and against all
authorities and powers in societies and in cultures.

Religious liberty as a human right was actualized in history primarily through this stream of thought. Professor
Sidney Mead correctly pointed out that religious freedom
in the American context was adopted largely as the result
of the necessity of the circumstances plus the efforts of
the political leaders of the Enlightenment.[12] To be sure,
the examples of Rhode Island, Pennsylvania, and certain
of the other middle colonies provided salutory examples.
But the fact remains that the grounds for the actions of
Williams and Penn were religious and not primarily political.[13] The former built on a concept of the two realms,
which had a long Christian history but which was never
brought to bear in relation to the question of religious
freedom. Penn built on the concept of the light within and
the impossibility of distorting or coercing it. Only men
such as Jefferson, Madison, and Franklin developed an
elaborate theory in terms of which they fought for and
won religious liberty on the American scene. Mead points
out that the Pietists and certain other religious groups in
American made common cause with the Enlightenment
thinkers at the time of the Constitution; however, once
religious liberty was attained, they turned with a vengeance upon the Enlightenment tradition.[14]

The Founding Fathers believed, then, that religion was
one of the most important of the natural rights and that
it was inalienable, or unchangeable. James Madison said,
"Because we hold it for a fundamental and undeniable
truth that religion is a duty that we owe to our Creator,
the manner of discharging it be directed only by reason

and conviction, not by force or violence." He indicated that "this right is, in its nature, an inalienable right." [15]

Jefferson pointed out in his concluding paragraph of "An Act for Establishing Religious Freedom" that though his particular legislature could not bind future legislatures, his own group was free to declare "and do declare that the rights hereby asserted are of the natural rights of mankind, and that if any act shall be hereinafter passed to repeal or to narrow its operation, such act will be an infringement of natural right." [16] He stated in his "Notes on Virginia": "Our rulers can have such authority over such natural rights only as we have submitted to them. The rights of conscience we never submitted, we could not submit. We are answerable for them to our God. The legitimate powers of government extend to such acts only as they are injurious to others. But it does me no injury for my neighbor to say there are twenty gods or no God." [17]

Furthermore, Jefferson and Madison were typical of the Enlightenment generation in stating that the free pursuit of religion leads only to truth. Jefferson stated: "The truth is great and will prevail if left to herself, that she is the proper and sufficient antagonist to error, and has nothing to fear from the conflict, unless by human interposition disarmed of her natural weapons free argument and debate, errors ceasing to be dangerous when it is permitted freely to contradict them." [18] Jefferson was convinced that if reason and free inquiry were used as the only agents against error, "they will support the true religion by bringing every false one to their tribunal, to the test of their investigation." [19]

It is clear that religious freedom as a human right can be and was defended on grounds developed during the

Enlightenment. From this perspective, two primary presuppositions upheld the possibility of religious freedom.
First, it was firmly believed that the free and unfettered
pursuit of the truth would not lead to chaos, but would
lead to a convergence on truth itself. This belief was possible because these men had an implicit faith in the essential harmony of the entire universe. A man of the Enlightenment could believe in the free activity and the
emergence of the maximum good of each individual in
every area of life, be it economics, politics, education,
philosophy, or religion, because of his unbounded faith
in the reality and the prevalence of underlying rationality
and harmony in the universe.

A second basic presupposition with which they func-
tioned was a particular definition of the nature of religion.
It is not necessary to go into the five so-called basic beliefs
of deism; however, they do summarize neatly the religious
beliefs of the Enlightenment.[20] God was identified with a
certain conception of reason and of ethics. All elements of
mystery, transcendence, and infinity were totally removed.
God was as predictable and understandable as any of the
other laws of nature because He was, in fact, the author
of all such laws, and they most fully expressed his nature.
One of the ironies of American history is that most
churches on the American scene have adopted religious
liberty as a principle and even as a natural human right,
but have rejected almost in toto the Enlightenment's conception of man, nature, and God. Meanwhile, they have
not developed any theory comparable to that held by the
Enlightenment as a defense of the natural rights theory
or as a defense of religious freedom as a human right.[21]

It is obvious that religious freedom as a human right can be defended from a wide variety of perspectives. It is not necessary to hold the eighteenth-century concept of God, implicit harmony in the universe, the *philosophes'* view of nature, of history, or of religion in order to argue purely from human reason for the fundamental right of freedom of religion. A very strong argument could be made on historical grounds simply, employing either pragmatism as a philosophical movement or employing arguments from history. Perhaps one of the most fruitful ways to defend religious liberty as an essential right would be to argue from the perspective provided by the modern concern for and analysis of the self, or the perspective provided by depth psychology. These could be used independently or they could be coordinated, but, in either case, a very strong defense could be made for the absolute necessity of religious freedom from a strictly rational analysis of human nature and history.

The basic problem is to analyze human nature, man, in such a way that his humanity is left inviolable. Christianity does this from a number of perspectives that build primarily on revelation or on various syntheses of reason and revelation. The problem is to define and defend man's humanity, his uniqueness, and his responsibilities from a position that does not receive its explicit presuppositions or orientation from a Christian point of view. To be sure, most Western thought implicitly involves a Judeo-Christian influence, but that is not the point. The point is to find a view of man that by its own nature appears persuasive, formative, and true for vast numbers of people, religious or nonreligious. That is what the eighteenth-century

view, that of natural rights, accomplished in large segments
of the Western world.

A good deal of modern thought centers on the problem
of the self and the intricate relationship between the self
and society. The fundamental problems discussed by psychology, sociology, anthropology, political science, and
even by much of contemporary theology reflect this situation. The Vatican schema on religious freedom correctly
brings to the foreground human dignity as the overwhelming concern of modern man. It is evident that the analysis
of inalienable rights, including religious freedom as a
human right, can no longer be understood or defended on
the grounds of the eighteenth-century view of nature and
of man.

The analysis of man, nature, and history undertaken by
such men as Buber, Tillich, Jung, and Reinhold and H.
Richard Niebuhr, to name but several, gives promise of
providing a new base on which to build a defense of certain "inalienable" freedoms that does justice both to the
uniqueness and freedom of man and to his involvement
with and responsibilities for his fellow men. For all of these
men, the analysis of the self, profoundly influenced by
existentialism and depth psychology, provides the point of
departure.

The thoroughgoing shift marked by this development
is from a concern for humanity in general, or for the
universal principles that define the human, to a concern
for the self as immediately experienced by the self. The
shift did not represent a turning away from social responsibility or from the search for that which is universally
true about man. On the contrary, it sought to find for
man authentically human and social relationships that

become possible only when the self is understood in its own uniqueness and manifold dimensions.

Buber's profound and brilliant analysis of the "I-Thou" relationship is one of the clearest and most creative examples.[22] Tillich's third volume of *Systematics* contains an extensive and seminal presentation of self-actualization of life and its ambiguities.[23] Both Niebuhrs wrote a book on the self as being of fundamental importance for an understanding of history and moral philosophy.[24] It is impossible to summarize or to detail the content and consequence of this effort in these few pages. It is necessary, however, to raise the question of its total significance to the problem of religious liberty as a human right.

The first thing that stands out is a totally different view of human and of right. The human is not defined primarily as an individual who possesses rational capacities that are but reflections of the rational structure of the universe. Nor is man defined primarily as a political animal. Man is defined as a centered self who is actualized in an ever-renewed series of relationships. The shift of emphasis is from a more or less static being defined by participation in certain rational categories to a being constantly realizing himself in a dialectical process of relationships.

Buber states that "through the thou a man becomes I." [25] If a man's relationship is never more than an I-It relationship, man never experiences fully his whole being, is never really fully self. But the dice appear loaded against the possibility of man having or maintaining an I-Thou relationship. All pressure is in the opposite direction. Buber states that it is "the exalted melancholy of our fate that every Thou in our world must become an It." [26] The possibility of an I-Thou relationship is exceedingly difficult to maintain, yet only through the I-Thou relationship can one become and remain authentically human.

At this point one could argue that to be human and to remain human every effort must be made to keep open the possibility of I-Thou relationships. Clearly, religion is one of the most important elements in life that encourages and makes possible such a relationship. Without the I-Thou relationship there is no genuine religion, though even in religion the relationship is constantly turning into an I-It relationship. This in no way undercuts or devaluates the role and significance of religion; rather it argues for the absolute necessity of freedom for the practice of religion in order to maximize the possibility of an I-Thou encounter. One thing is clear: if man is forced to believe and act in religion in a prescribed way, he is doomed to an I-It relationship. By definition, the I-Thou relationship must be free of all coercion and compulsion. To have a true religious experience, man must have religious freedom. If one only becomes fully human through the fleeting yet constantly renewed I-Thou relationship, then man's humanity demands religious freedom for the possibility of such encounters. Political or social control of religion deprives man of his right to genuine religiousness and to genuine humanity.

If it is true that the self and not nature is the point of departure for understanding man, then religious liberty as a human right must be grounded in some understanding of the self. That is the only way it can be viewed by modern man as an inalienable right, a right that man, if he wishes to become and remain man, cannot surrender. Man lives through dialogue. He has been described by some as the answerer, one who responds to questions about self, world, and nature.[27] Such a response is always in relation to others, both past and present. A genuine answer is itself a relationship that takes into the self that which has been presented by others. Again, this demonstrates both the centrality of the self, the centered out of which it responds, and, at the same time, the inevitable involvement of the self with others before it can be the self. The social character of life is not to be affirmed simply as a logical necessity; it is experienced immediately by the person or self in an encounter with the world and with other persons.

From this point of view, a base is provided to reject all pretensions to absolute power on the part of the state or society. Nevertheless, room remains for a proper evaluation of the state and of society. It becomes possible to elaborate a series of rights for the individual that no state can grant or take away. These so-called rights are to be seen as integral to the realization and the sustenance of the self. Without the exercise of these rights it becomes impossible or exceedingly difficult for a person to actualize his self or to truly participate with others in creative personal or in responsible social relationships. Thus, human rights are grounded in the uniqueness and the particularity of all selves, and not in the fact that each man participates in and reflects an abstract ideal. Each man is sacred not because he partakes in certain universal principles that cannot be violated, but simply because he *is*. He is a unique self, himself, with the potentialities and responsibilities of realizing his self in relation to others. To do this man requires freedom of speech, of the press, of discussion, and of religion.

The schema on the freedom of religion properly stresses

human dignity as one of the bases for religious liberty. A number of philosophers could be employed to give content and specific meaning to that phrase. Thomism, Kantianism, eighteenth-century natural rights philosophy, day-to-day human affirmations built through historical precedents—all of these can be employed to make sense of this human dignity that requires certain inalienable rights. Perhaps, as modern men, we are presented with a new alternative to defend human rights. It has just begun to emerge in its strength and power. Juridical distinctions are absolutely necessary to make explicit the civic protection of this right, but a commonly shared perspective and set of presuppositions concerning man, society, and the state underlie all effective juridical distinctions and judgments. Western man again is in search for such a view of man. A number of views are beginning to converge on this problem. They appear capable of articulating a fresh, new, vigorous conception of human rights, including that of religious liberty.

NOTES

1. *The Decree on Ecumenism* (Glen Rock, New Jersey: The Paulist Press, 1965). Section 4, p. 55; section 7, p. 60; section 10, p. 63; section 12, p. 64.

2. *Declaration on the Relation of the Church to Non-Christian Religions*. Section 1. "In this age of ours, when day by day mankind is being drawn closer together, and the ties between various peoples are becoming stronger, the Church con-

siders more attentively her relationship to non-Christian religions. In her task of promoting unity and love among men, indeed among nations, she above all considers in this declaration what men have in common and what leads to mutual fellowship." Section 2, "The Catholic Church rejects nothing that is true and holy in these religions. . . . The Church, therefore, exhorts her sons, that through dialogue and collaboration with the followers of other religions . . . they recognize, preserve, and promote those spiritual and moral goods as well as those socio-cultural values found among those men." Cf. sections 4 and 5.

3. *Ibid.*, section 5.

4. *Pastoral Constitution on the Church in the Modern World* (Huntington, Indiana: Our Sunday Visitor Inc., 1965). Section 3, p. 4; section 16, p. 15; section 17, pp. 15-16, 26, section 21, pp. 18-19, section 23, p. 23; section 24, p. 23; section 25, p. 24; section 26, pp. 24-25; section 27, p. 25; section 28, p. 26; section 29, pp. 26-27; section 31, p. 28; section 40, p. 38; section 41, pp. 38-39; section 42, p. 40; section 43, pp. 41-42; section 44, pp. 42-43; section 55, p. 56; section 58, pp. 59-60; section 73, p. 73; section 74, p. 75; section 76, pp. 76-77; section 90, p. 90; section 92, p. 91.

5. *Declaration on Religious Freedom* (Washington, D.C.: National Catholic Welfare Conference, 1956). Section 2, pp. 2-3; section 6, p. 6.

6. Perry Miller, "The Contributions of the Protestant Churches to Religious Liberty in Colonial America," in *Church History*, IV (March, 1935), pp. 57 ff.

7. Carl L. Becker, *The Heavenly City of the Eighteenth Century Philosphers* (New Haven: Yale University Press, 1932), pp. 47 ff. Cf. also, Ernst Cassirer, *The Philosophy of the Enlightenment* (Princeton: Princeton University Press, 1951), pp. 37 ff; pp. 234 ff.

8. E. Cassierer, *op. cit.*, pp. 253 ff.

9. Benjamin F. Wright, *American Interpretations of Natural Law* (Cambridge: Harvard University Press, 1931), pp. 124-148. Ralph Barton Perry, *Puritanism and Democracy* (New York: Vanguard Press, 1944), pp. 117-137, 147-174.

10. Becker, *op. cit.*, pp. 43, 48, 413-422, 438-469, 479-489.

11. E. Cassirer, *op. cit.*, pp. 168 ff.

12. Sidney E. Mead, *The Lively Experiment* (New York: Harper & Row, 1963), pp. 16-71.

13. Anson P. Stokes, *Church and State in the United States* (New York: Harper & Brothers, 1950, (first edition), I, 194-202, 206-208.

14. Sidney E. Mead, *op. cit.*, pp. 41 ff., 55 ff.

15. James Madison, "A Memorial and Remonstrance on the Religious Rights of Man" in *Cornerstones of Religious Freedom in America*, ed. Joseph L. Blau (Boston: Beacon Press, 1949), p. 81.

16. Thomas Jefferson, "An Act for Establishing Religious Freedom," *op. cit.*, p. 75.

17. Thomas Jefferson, "Notes on Virginia. Query XVII. The Different Religions Received into that State," *op. cit.*, p. 78.

18. Thomas Jefferson, "An Act for Establishing Religious Freedom," *op. cit.*, p. 75.

19. Thomas Jefferson, "Notes on Virginia," *op. cit.*, p. 78.

20. Benjamin Franklin, *Representative Selections*, eds. Frank L. Mott and Chester E. Jorgenson (New York: American Book Co., 1936), pp. 69-70.

21. Sidney E. Mead, *op. cit.*, pp. 66-71, 108-115, 127-129, 139-142.

22. Martin Buber, *I and Thou* (Edinburgh: T. & T. Clark, 1950).

23. Paul Tillich, *Systematic Theology* (Chicago: University of Chicago Press), III, 30-106.

24. H. Richard Niebuhr, *The Responsible Self* (New York: Harper & Row, 1963), Reinhold Niebuhr, *The Self and the Drama of History* (New York: Scribner's, 1955).

25. Martin Buber, *op. cit.*, pp. 28 ff.

26. *Ibid.*, p. 16.

27. H. Richard Niebuhr, *op. cit.*, pp. 56 ff.

The Catholic Concept
of Religious Freedom
as a Human Right

FRANCIS J. CANAVAN, S.J.

AN essay on the Catholic concept of religious freedom
as a human right would seem, at the present time, to be
a somewhat otiose undertaking. Since the fourth and final
session of Vatican Council II there exists a clear, concise,
and highly authoritative statement on the subject, the
Council's Declaration on Religious Freedom. (All references to the declaration in this paper are to the text as
found in *The Documents of Vatican II*, edited by Walter
M. Abbott, S.J., and published by the Guild Press, Herder
& Herder, and the Association Press, New York, 1966.)
A presentation of the Catholic view of religious freedom
today can only summarize, explain, and, perhaps, criticize
the Council's declaration. It cannot take its place and no
reader would be well advised to substitute a commentary
for a study of the text of the declaration itself.

The document consists of a preamble and two chapters,

and is further divided into continuously numbered sections. Chapter 1 develops the idea of religious freedom as it is known by reason, and presents what is the document's basic argument for religious freedom. Chapter 2, while acknowledging that divine revelation does not affirm in so many words the right to religious freedom as defined here, reviews those scriptural texts that cast "further light . . . on the general principles upon which the doctrine of this Declaration on Religious Freedom is based" (article 9). Since we are concerned with the concept of religious freedom and not with its scriptural foundations, this essay will confine itself to the preamble and chapter 1.

The opening sentence of the declaration lays the foundation of its doctrine of religious freedom as a human right. It reads: "A sense of the dignity of the human person has been impressing itself more and more deeply on the consciousness of contemporary man." The Council intends to affirm religious freedom as a human right, founded on the dignity of the human person. As John Courtney Murray, S.J., points out in his notes on the declaration (footnote 5), the document nowhere uses the phrase for which the phrase frequently stands, namely, that I have a right to do what my conscience tells me to do, simply because my conscience tells me to do it. The dignity of the human person, as conceived by the Council, is an objective moral reality, not a subjective belief, sentiment, or conviction held by any individual or group. "Therefore," the declaration affirms in a later passage, "the right to religious freedom has its foundation, not in the subjective disposition of the person, but in his very nature" (article 2).

On the other hand, the Council acknowledges that it finds this objective moral reality in its historical evolution in the consciousness of modern man. In modern history men have become more and more deeply aware of the dignity of the human person and consequently have made certain demands, which the preamble of the declaration states in these terms: "that men should act on their own judgment, enjoying and making use of a responsible freedom, not driven by coercion but motivated by a sense of duty" and "that constitutional limits should be set to the powers of government, in order that there may be no encroachment on the rightful freedom of the person and of associations." "This demand for freedom in human society . . . regards, in the first place, the free exercise of religion in human society."

It is no secret that the demand for the free exercise of religion in modern times was in large part first made outside the Catholic Church and against her status as the one legally permitted religion in many countries, and that the Church reacted to this demand with deep scepticism, when not with outright hostility. But today, the Declaration on Religious Freedom informs us: "This Vatican Council takes careful note of these desires in the minds of men. It proposes to declare them to be greatly in accord with truth and justice. To this end, it searches into the sacred tradition and doctrine of the Church—the treasury out of which the Church continually brings forth new things that are in harmony with the things that are old."

Unless we are prepared to subscribe to the liberal myth of progress, or to affirm with Hegel that the real is the rational and the rational is the real, we cannot assume that every belief that emerges in the historical consciousness of modern man affirms a genuine human value and establishes a valid human right. But the Council declares that the claim to the free exercise of religion in society, founded on a growing sense of the dignity of the human person, is "greatly in accord with truth and justice" and is, in fact, a natural human right. Out of the conflict and controversy of the past several centuries, so much of it directed against the Catholic Church, there has emerged a refined awareness of a universal right to religious freedom that the Church today accepts and affirms as valid in itself and as being in accordance with her own doctrine.

The declaration is careful to state, in the remaining paragraphs of its preamble, that religious freedom "has to do with immunity from coercion in civil society." Therefore, the declaration concludes, "it leaves untouched traditional Catholic doctrine on the moral duty of men and societies toward the true religion and toward the one Church of Christ."

In an article in the November 20, 1965, issue of *America*, the present writer criticized the choice of the language in the last sentence above on the ground that "it puzzles and annoys non-Catholics" to be told that they have a "moral duty" to the Catholic Church. It is unnecessary to repeat here everything said in that article; the essential point is that the declaration contains no hint of compulsion to be exercised on non-Catholics and intends only to make it clear that, it sincerely and unequivocally affirming the right to religious freedom, the Church does not mean to renounce or diminish her claim to be the one Church of Christ. It should also be remarked that the Church claims freedom for herself on the ground of the divine mandate given to her by Christ himself, in addition to the general ground of the dignity of the human person (article 13).

The heart of the declaration's analysis of religious freedom is found in chapter 1, articles 2 and 3. First, the document defines its subject in general terms: "This freedom means that all men are to be immune from coercion on the part of individuals or of social groups and of human power, in such wise that no one is to be forced to act in a manner contrary to his own beliefs, whether privately or publicly, whether alone or in association with others, within due limits." Secondly, the declaration states: "This right of the human person to religious freedom is to be recognized in the constitutional law whereby society is governed; thus it is to become a civil right."

The document then asserts that the natural and civil right to religious freedom derives from the natural obligation to seek religious truth, to adhere to it when found and to order one's whole life in accordance with its demands. Both the right and the obligation are consequences of men's nature as "beings endowed with reason and free will and therefore privileged to bear personal responsibility." The right to religious freedom follows from the obligation to seek and live by religious truth in this manner: "Men cannot discharge these obligations in a manner in keeping with their own nature unless they enjoy immunity from external coercion as well as psychological freedom."

The Catholic case for religious freedom thus does not in any way rest on the proposition that human reason or conscience is a law unto itself. On the contrary, it supposes that "the highest norm of human life is the divine law—eternal, objective and universal—whereby God orders, directs and governs the entire universe and all the ways of the human community." "Wherefore," the declaration argues, "every man has the duty, and therefore the right, to seek the truth in matters religious."

It is clear, too, that the Council's argument for religious freedom does not at all imply that religious truth and error are indistinguishable, or that one is free to choose truth or error indifferently. The entire argument depends on the obligation to seek and adhere to the truth, which alone can found rights.

But, the declaration notes, "as the truth is discovered, it is by a personal assent that men are to adhere to it." This assertion introduces the subjective element of conscience. In its final and promulgated form, the Declaration on Religious Freedom nowhere distinguishes between the erroneous and the true conscience, as earlier drafts did. It speaks only of conscience *tout court* and argues directly from the obligation to follow conscience to the right to do so.

In the declaration's own words: "On his part, man perceives and acknowledges the imperatives of the divine law through the mediation of conscience. In all this activity a man is bound to follow his conscience, in order that he may come to God, the end and purpose of life. It follows that he is not to be forced to act in a manner contrary to his conscience. Nor, on the other hand, is he to be constrained from acting in accordance with his conscience, especially in matters religious."

The document draws from the obligation to serve God by following conscience a universal human right to religious freedom. Every man has this right, even if he does not "live up to his obligation of seeking the truth and adhering to it; and the exercise of this right is not to be impeded, provided that the just requirements of public order are observed." The argument thus starts from the most universal and fundamental human need, the need "to come to God, the end and purpose of life." It translates this need into the obligation to follow conscience, and derives from it a subordinate and related need: immunity from coercion to act contrary to conscience or to refrain from acting in accordance with conscience. Since the need is objective and universal, the right to freedom in matters of conscience, and especially in matters religious, is likewise objective and universal.

It will be noted that this argument is very much in the rational, natural-law tradition of Catholic thought. The document does not use the term "natural law," but it posits a universal human nature, whose natural tendencies and needs are knowable to the human mind. It further assumes the existence of God, who is truth, and the truth about whom answers to the deepest of human needs. By rational analysis of the relationship between God and man it concludes that religious freedom is a natural human right.

Now, if all men sought and infallibly found religious truth, the question of religious freedom would not arise. It is precisely because men's beliefs about religious truth vary so widely and so deeply, and because their consciences are highly fallible, that the coercion of some persons by others in matters religious is possible and, in fact, takes place. In asserting the right of all men to immunity from this coercion, the Declaration on Religious Freedom proclaims neither the right to be wrong nor the impossibility of distinguishing truth from error in religion. By a seeming paradox, it guarantees the possibility of being wrong in matters religious, without therefore suffering coercion, as an objective requirement of the nature of free and responsible persons who were made by God to know the truth about Him. Fr. Murray's comment is apposite here: "Neither error nor evil can be the object of a right, only what is true and good. It is, however, true and good that a man should enjoy freedom from coercion in matters religious" (footnote 5).

The Council's argument for religious freedom is thus in no way tinged with agnosticism or subjectivism; it is expressed in the language of a realistic, not of a nominalistic, philosophy. Unfortunately, however acceptable the conclusion that all men have a right to religious freedom, this way of arriving at it is not one that is likely to commend itself to many minds outside the natural-law tradition. It does not follow, of course, that the Council was wrong in its choice of language. It was concerned both to set the case for religious freedom on what it considered to be a firm foundation and to assimilate a newly asserted right into the Catholic tradition, of which natural law forms so significant a part.

The declaration proceeds in the same vein to assert religious freedom as a social, not merely an individual, right. "The social nature of man itself requires that he should give external expression to his internal acts of religion; that he should share with others in matters religious; that he should profess his religion in community. Injury, therefore, is done to the human person and to the very order established by God for human life, if the free exercise of religion is denied in society, provided that the just requirements of public order are observed." Two paragraphs below, in article 4, it states: "Religious communities are a requirement of the social nature both of man and of religion itself." The argument, it will be noted again, is from nature, that is, from man's nature as not only a free and responsible being, but also a social being.

Articles 4 and 5 of the declaration enunciate a number

of detailed freedoms that religious communities (churches, in the broadest sense of the term) must enjoy in order to have religious freedom in practice. It is unnecessary to recite them all here. But, in summary, the Council claims for all churches, as for the Catholic Church, the right to conduct public worship, to instruct their members, to have their own institutions, and to govern themselves. The latter right specifically includes freedom to select, train, appoint, and transfer their ministers; also to own their own property and to communicate freely with religious authorities and communities abroad.

On what has been a sensitive point in some Latin Catholic countries, the Council proclaims the right of religious communities "not to be hindered in their public teaching and witness to their faith" or of "freely undertaking to show the special value of their doctrine in what concerns the organization of society and the inspiration of the whole of human activity." It notes, however, that right would be abused by the kind of proselytism that "might seem to carry a hint of coercion" or by the "kind of persuasion that would be dishonorable or unworthy, especially when dealing with poor or uneducated people."

In article 5, the declaration devotes a paragraph to the family's right to religious freedom. This includes the right "freely to live its own domestic religious life under the guidance of parents" and the right of the parents to determine "the kind of religious education that their children are to receive." Certain obligations consequently fall upon government. It must not force children to receive instruction that is not in accordance with their religious beliefs, or impose on all a single system of education from which all religious formation is excluded. Indeed, government must not impose "unjust burdens on parents, whether directly or indirectly" that would prevent them from making a "genuinely free choice of schools" for their children. It may be remarked that, if this paragraph implicitly censures the educational policies of Communist states, it also censures those of the United States.

The declaration takes up the limits of religious freedom in article 7. "Society has the right to defend itself against possible abuses committed on pretext of freedom of religion. It is the special duty of government to provide this protection." In all the discussion of religious freedom in the Council, it was never questioned that this freedom, like all other freedoms, can be abused and that government has the right to control such abuse. But great concern was felt about the norm or standard by which government would distinguish between the abuse of religious freedom and the legitimate free exercise of religion.

The term first used in drafts of the declaration, "the common good," was felt to afford too much latitude to governments in restricting the religious activities of citizens. The final text of the declaration, therefore, consistently uses "the just requirements of public order" as the sole limitation on the free exercise of religion. Even this term, of course, is open to abuse by governments, but the declaration tries to explain in as precise terms as it can what it means by public order.

First, it says: "Government is not to act in arbitrary fashion or in an unfair spirit of partisanship." This sentence recognizes that, in any rational system of law, it is not the exercise of authority for the common welfare that violates freedom, but the arbitrary and partisan use of power. Government's action against abuses of religious freedom, therefore, "is to be controlled by juridical norms which are in conformity with the objective moral order."

Just as the declaration tried to derive religious freedom from the objective moral order by asserting it to be an objectively valid and universal natural right, so it attempts to restrict government's right to limit the free exercise of religion by subjecting governmental power to the "objective moral order." The term, admittedly, is offensive to many; it sounds like an attempt to smuggle in Catholic moral theology under the guise of natural law. The question is immediately asked: Who is to determine what the objective moral order is? Yet it must also be admitted that religious freedom can be abused to the point where it becomes harmful to other persons and to society in general, and that it is government's duty to restrain such abuses. In appealing to the "objective moral order" the conciliar document is only trying to establish the legal norms for limiting the free exercise of religion on a basis that is as independent of the whim of governments as it is of the vagaries of the persons who use religious freedom as a justification for offenses against their fellow men.

The Council's intention emerges clearly from its explanation of the "juridical norms which are in conformity with the objective moral order." "These norms," it says, "arise out of the need for effective safeguard of the rights of all citizens and for peaceful settlement of conflicts of rights; also out of the need for an adequate care of genuine public peace, which comes about when men live together in good order and in true justice; and finally out of the need for a proper guardianship of public morality. These matters constitute the basic component of the common welfare: they are what is meant by public order."

That is to say, the objective moral order, which is not subject to the will of men, prescribes the protection of rights, public peace, and public morality as fundamental purposes of human society. To realize and safeguard these purposes is to establish and maintain public order. In enforcing "the just requirements of public order" government does not act arbitrarily or violate religious freedom, even if it prevents people from doing things that their religious beliefs authorize or perhaps even command (ritual murder, sacred prostitution, and polygamy are extreme, but not fantastic, examples).

The declaration does not answer the question: Who is to determine what the objective moral order is? But, at least under a constitutional form of government (which the declaration seems to consider normal), the moral order and the public order derived from it will be effective restraints on government insofar as they are accepted by the collective conscience of the larger and sounder part of society and are upheld by constitutional organs, such as the courts of law. There is nothing in the Declaration on Religious Freedom that furnishes grounds for the suspicion that it really contemplates a Catholic dictatorship repressing heresy under the guise of upholding the "objective moral order." On the contrary, having explained what it means by the public order, the declaration concludes: "For the rest, the usages of society are to be the usages of freedom in their full range: that is, the freedom of man is to be respected as far as possible and is not to be curtailed except when and in so far as necessary."

It was remarked above that the document seems to consider constitutional government as normal. We have already said that, in its preamble, it notes and approves the demand "increasingly made" today that "men should act on their own judgment, enjoying and making use of a responsible freedom" and that "constitutional limits should be set to the powers of government." Among the essential characteristics of constitutional government are that it is limited in its powers and that it is responsible to those whom it governs. It cannot be said that the declaration advocates constitutional government in this passage, but it certainly shows a bias in that direction.

The limitations of governmental power are again stressed in the final paragraph of article 3, which declares: "Government ought indeed to take account of the religious life of the people and show it favor, since the function of government is to make provision for the common welfare. However, it would clearly transgress the limits set to its power were it to presume to command or inhibit acts that are religious."

But it is in article 6 that the declaration deals most fully with government's duties in regard to religious freedom. The common welfare, it says, "chiefly consists in the protection of the rights, and in the performance of the duties, of the human person." Since the common welfare is the concern of the whole society, "the care of the right to religious freedom devolves upon the people as a whole, upon social groups, upon government, and upon the Church and other religious communities, in virtue of the duty of all toward the common welfare, and in the manner proper to each." But it is "among the essential duties of government" in particular to safeguard "the religious freedom of all its citizens."

The declaration does not proscribe the "establishment" of a particular church or religion as contrary per se to religious freedom. On the other hand, it in no way upholds establishment as an ideal and, indeed, grants it only a rather reluctant recognition as an historical fact. "If, in view of peculiar circumstances obtaining among certain peoples, special legal recognition is given to one religious community in the constitutional order of society, it is at the same time imperative that the right of all citizens and religious communities to religious freedom should be recognized and made effective."

"Finally," the document declares, "government is to see to it that the equality of citizens before the law, which is itself an element of the common welfare, is never violated, whether openly or covertly, for religious reasons. Nor is there to be discrimination among citizens." It may be remarked that the equality of citizens before the law is another essential characteristic of constitutional government as it is understood in the world today.

The present writer agrees with the criticism made by Professor Franklin H. Littell in his "Response" to the Declaration on Religious Freedom. He says: "In one major dimension, the logic of religious freedom remains undeveloped. The theme is thoroughly elaborated in reference to the natural rights of persons and associations. It is soundly grounded in the system of belief of the Church. The implications for the nature of a just government are less thoroughly treated. Governments which persecute are not only defying the rule of reason and the law of the gospel, however: they are also guilty of denying the limits and style of sound government."

We have been at pains to point out the passages in which the declaration indicates its acceptance of the idea of constitutional government. Yet it is regrettable that this idea was not thoroughly developed and made a major basis of the case for religious freedom. This writer must confess that he is not entirely convinced by the document's argument, which proceeds from the obligation to follow conscience to a rather elaborate series of rights that collectively constitute religious freedom. Does this argument really bear the full weight that is put on it? To say that it may not do so is not to lessen in any way the Council's commitment of the Church to the cause of religious freedom. It is only to suggest that the commitment might have had a stronger intellectual underpinning if it had devoted more attention to the nature of a just political and legal order in human society.

In other words, the declaration might have done better to continue along the line of thought that it began in its preamble. There, having remarked that men today increasingly demand a responsible freedom and, consequently, constitutional limits on the powers of government, it says: "This Vatican Council takes careful note of these desires in the minds of men. It proposes to declare them to be greatly in accord with truth and justice" and with the doctrine of the Church. There would have been several advantages in developing this proposition.

It would have avoided treating religious freedom in isolation from other fundamental civil liberties. It would also have avoided proposing too abstract an argument for religious freedom. Instead, it would have put the Church in the position of ratifying, as an exigence of reason consonant with Catholic doctrine, the basic notions of constitutional government and civil liberty (including religious freedom) that have evolved in our time. The Council's statement on religious freedom would thus have been more fully in line with the social teaching of the modern popes, who have increasingly emphasized the human person with all his rights as the foundation and the end of civil society.

It would also have situated the argument for religious freedom in the stream of history. Without abandoning the idea of human nature as a moral norm or denying the need to found human rights on the objective moral order, it would have recognized more clearly that human nature unfolds itself—and therefore progressively recognizes its duties and rights—only in the course of time. Finally, by squarely basing its case for religious freedom on men's growing consciousness of their dignity and rights, the declaration would have proposed an argument more easily comprehensible by and acceptable to the mass of people today.

It cannot be said that this line of argument is not found in the Declaration on Religious Freedom; but it is not adequately developed and is neglected in favor of an abstract ethical argument. The defect, if such it be, is hardly fatal, however. In this regard, we may be pardoned for again quoting Fr. Murray (the author's dependence on whom must already by obvious). He says: "It was necessary for the Council to present an argument for the principle of religious freedom, lest anyone should mistakenly think that the Church was accepting religious freedom merely on pragmatic grounds or as a concession to contemporary circumstances. However, it was not the intention of the Council to affirm that the argument, as made in the text, is final and decisive. Complete and systematic study of the arguments for religious freedom is a task left to the scholars of the Church, working in ecumenical spirit with scholars of no religious communities, and in humanist spirit with scholars of no religious convictions who are concerned with the exigencies of human dignity. The Council merely presents certain lines or elements of argument" (footnote 7). With this call to further work it is fitting to conclude an all too sketchy analysis of the Catholic concept of religious freedom as a human right.

PART III

RELIGIOUS FREEDOM
AND THE CHRISTIAN REVELATION

Religious Freedom and
the Old Testament

DAVID NOEL FREEDMAN

No one with an awareness of the history of the Christian Church could fail to be moved by the drama of Vatican Council II, not least in its forthright declaration on religious freedom. Who could have thought twenty years ago, or even ten, that such a statement would be formally proclaimed under the seal of the Pope and the assembled bishops of the Catholic communion? Those of us who have watched the Council in its deliberations and actions with attentive interest and growing enthusiasm can only be thankful for the manifest grace of God in guiding the Council, and can only applaud the fathers of the Church for their courage and willingness to move with the leading of the Holy Spirit, especially in the area of religious freedom. For it is clear that this affirmation is at once the presupposition and objective of the proclamation of the Gospel, as well as providing the necessary and indispensable framework for the ecumenical dialogue now taking place. Only in an atmosphere of liberty, free of any taint of coercion from without or within, can Biblical faith truly prosper and the reunion of separated brethren be contemplated and promoted.

The topic selected for my presentation is "Religious Freedom and the Christian Revelation." Since I am to share the title with my esteemed colleague and close friend, Fr. John L. McKenzie, I will seize what little advantage there may be in making the initial presentation by choosing that smaller segment of the whole that is more congenial to my interest, and, incidentally, the only area in which I could claim any competence, namely the Old Testament and its bearing on the subject of religious freedom. I confess, however, that I feel a little like those innumerable prophets of Baal at Mt. Carmel, who were persuaded by Elijah to enter the competition first, while he took the more modest second but devastatingly effective counterpunching position. The melancholy consequences for the frontrunners need not be rehearsed here.

There is a statement in the document before us concerning the relationship of religious freedom to revelation, which will serve as a point of contact and departure for us: "Revelation does not indeed affirm in so many words the right of man to immunity from external coercion in matters religious" (article 9). The statement occurs in a paragraph in which it is affirmed that the doctrine of religious freedom is entirely consistent with revelation. ". . . This doctrine of freedom has roots in divine revelation. . . . It is therefore completely in accord with the nature of faith that in matters religious every manner of coercion on the part of men should be excluded" (articles

9–10). The argument is developed by citing the example of Jesus and his followers in promoting the Gospel and enlisting men in the community of faith. A number of passages from the New Testament are quoted or mentioned in support of the contention that, in matters religious, Jesus and his followers did not have recourse to coercive authority (a single passage of the Old Testament, Isa. 42:1–4, is used as a description of Jesus' activity in this regard). While we should be and are in hearty agreement with the inferences drawn concerning religious freedom, we may be less certain of the exegetical propriety of the interpretation placed on the New Testament passages, and even more dubious of their applicability to the question of religious freedom. But leaving that problem to the attention of someone better able to handle it, like my successor, let us turn to the Old Testament, which, as we pointed out, has been left untouched in the declaration. On the basis of this fact it might be supposed or inferred that there is nothing in the Old Testament that bears on the question. In point of fact the opposite is true: almost everything does. The Old Testament simply teems with relevant data arising out of concrete historical situations in which the issue of religious freedom figures prominently. There is an acute problem of selection and organization, as well as of interpretation and evaluation, but not of the lack of pertinent material.

Not having heard the full story of the nine editions of the declaration, I can only guess as to the reasons for the systematic exclusion of the Old Testament. There has always been a marked tendency in the Church to slight or pass over the Old Testament on the bland assumption that it has been displaced by the New Testament. This is one of the oldest heresies in the history of the Church, but it has proved extremely tenacious and crops up in different forms in every generation. In any form, however, it reflects a misreading of the Bible and the false understanding of the New Testament itself. It is all the more ironic to find this situation in the Church at a time when archaeological discoveries have provided us with potent tools to unlock the secrets of the Bible, enabling us to grasp its content and meaning with greater skill and better understanding than was possible in the past, and so to appreciate its continuity and essential unity.

Another and possibly more cogent consideration may be hidden in the assertion that the doctrine of religious freedom is consistent with revelation, which I take to include the Scriptures. As a matter of fact, it has long been widely held by students of the Bible that the Old Testament is not in agreement with this doctrine, and that neither religious freedom nor its common accompaniment, religious diversity, is really contemplated, much less approved, in the Old Testament. Thus, the lack of reference to the Old Testament could be explained on the grounds that the Old Testament had nothing positive to contribute to the doctrine of religious freedom. In other words, the fathers of the Council, having strong convictions about the validity and necessity of the doctrine, knew where they wanted to come out, but were considerably less certain about the argument from Scripture, especially the Old Testament. An effort was made to relate the doctrine to the New Testament, as we have seen, but the Old Testament was given up as a bad job, if the attempt was made at all.

Perhaps the matter should be dropped at this point, as

the bishops in their wisdom left it; and it may seem picayune to many to cavil at a matter of this kind. But it seems to me to be a valid expression of the spirit of religious freedom (though some may prefer to call it an example of Protestant anarchism) to suggest that the Biblical, specifically Old Testament, data is important for the discussion of the question, and could contribute both positively and negatively to a better understanding and formulation of the doctrine. It is first of all a matter of presenting the Biblical material squarely, and then of dealing with it constructively in the light of tradition and experience.

What is often regarded as the essential teaching of the Old Testament on the subject may be found in a typical passage dealing with the conquest of the land of Canaan (Deut. 7:1–5, 16 ff.). When the Israelites invade the land, they are to have no contact with the local inhabitants, but are to exterminate them. In the process, the religion of Canaan is to be ruthlessly suppressed in all its manifestations. Yahwism is to be the sole religion of the land and its people. There is to be no tolerance of religious diversity, no religious freedom. The imposition of Israelite religious obligations on alien residents (*gerim*) and slaves, as well as the enforcement of laws against mixed marriages (involving people of different religious communities) in the days of Ezra and Nehemiah, only strengthen the case. Apparent exceptions to these rules, like the construction of shrines dedicated to pagan deities by Solomon, and the encouragement of Baal worship in the days of Ahab and Jezebel, are roundly denounced by the prophets as violations of the basic terms of covenant religion. If this data does not exactly point in the direction of the doctrine of religious freedom, at least it may help to explain why the several churches, Catholic and Protestant, labored under the impression for centuries that they should go and do likewise.

Admittedly, the initial impression is rather a grim one for the doctrine of religious freedom, and we might well be tempted to look elsewhere for something more palatable to the modern taste, or more in keeping with what conscience unmistakably tells us is the necessary truth for our day. Before we do so, however, it might not be amiss to examine even this terrifying material more closely. Whether such an exercise is worthwhile will depend upon our attitude toward the Scriptures, but for those who believe that in its broad extent it is an authentic record of the experience of a people with its God, it becomes an imperative moral duty to investigate the whole matter further, not omitting the more distasteful data, but attempting to understand, if not wholly to accept it.

With regard to the doctrine of holy war enunciated in the book of Deuteronomy, it is to be noted that it has a limited application to a particular territory at a particular time, and that there is no basis at all for supposing that it is a universal warrant for wholesale slaughter. In addition, and this may seem like a macabre joke, there is actually no thought of conversion by force. It is nowhere suggested that conversion of the Canaanites is either an objective or an option. Their fate has been decided by God for an accumulation of crimes having nothing to do with Israel. Israel is simply the instrument of divine punishment, as the Assyrians and Babylonians were later in relation to Israel. It will be seen that the teaching of the Old Testament at this point is not incompatible with a doctrine of immunity from external coercion in religious matters. The Canaanites were a special case. The neighbors of Israel, with equally detestable religious beliefs and practices, were to be left in peace. The severe territorial limitation of the conquest ensured a world of religious diversity, and a host of nations free to decide their own religious faith and practice. The situation is accepted with equanimity by the Biblical historian, who regards it as a permanent feature of human history (cf. Deut. 4:19), a history ordained by God. Israel is not to interfere in any way with the religion of any other nation, but is to live peaceably in the midst of all. To be sure, the prophets speak of the judgment of God against nations that defy His law, and the hope is expressed that in the last days all nations will worship and serve the one true God. But these ends are not to be accomplished by Israel's imperial expansion, or any external coercion. It is to be emphasized that the freedom to order its religious life is extended not only to Israel, the community of the true faith, but to all other nations, in spite of the fact that their religious beliefs and practices are specifically and categorically branded as false. The only exception is the occupants of the Holy Land, whose tenure has been terminated by divine decree (cf. Deut. 9:4–5).

Historically, the independence of Israel, from the time of the Exodus, guaranteed the integrity of Israelite religion and protected it from external pressure or coercion. At the same time the power of the state was used to maintain uniform compliance to religious norms, thus restricting the religious freedom of the members of the community. No simple solution to the dilemma of the use of force has ever been devised, but the historical experience

of Israel led to a progressive loosening of the links
between civil power and the religious community, thus
allowing for the development of religious diversity and the
gradual abandonment of coercive power in matters religious. From the time of the Exile on, the Biblical community enjoyed a considerable measure of religious freedom in spite of the loss of political independence. In a
setting of this kind religious diversity was possible, and
during the last two centuries before the common era, a
number of different parties or sects appeared within
Judaism. The developing diversity within the Jewish community required attitudes of mutual tolerance, if not
acceptance and active cooperation. Thus, Rabbi Gamaliel
could express the classic doctrine of religious freedom in
opposing coercive action with respect to the nascent
Christian sect (cf. Acts 5:34–39, especially verse 38). The
Biblical data thus brings us to the New Testament witness
to the example and practice of Jesus and his disciples, who
lived and worked in a setting of religious diversity, which
reflected a significant measure of religious freedom. It was
the product of scriptural precedent and Jewish tradition,
for inevitably the way of the oppressed is the way to religious liberty.

There is another facet of the question that remains to
be considered: freedom within the religious community,
or the freedom of dissent. We have been speaking largely
of the freedom of the religious community from external
coercion, but not explicitly of the freedom of the individual within the religious community to diverge or dissent
from the consensus. By renouncing the use of force in
relation to the individual right of religious decision, the
declaration seems to protect the right of dissent in faith

and practice. But, in fact, this is not so, or as it has been so carefully explained to us, not yet so. This is in accordance with the practice of all religious communities, which rarely, if ever, permit dissent beyond minimal and peripheral variations from the established norms. Even without the help of coercive civil authority, religious communities have powerful weapons to compel conformity, such as the denial of sacred rites to the rebellious, and, ultimately, expulsion from the community. It is difficult to see how a religious community could survive without certain instruments of coercion. Whether these are conceived spiritually or materially, the effect is much the same; that they interfere with and infringe upon the religious liberty of the individual member of the community is undeniable.

The Old Testament acknowledges the authority of divine law and its appointed executors, as well as the coercive power available to the religious community. Violations of the basic standards of faith and practice were to be punished in summary fashion; whether by execution or expulsion is not always clear. There seemed to be little room for dissent, but there was at least one kind that deserves our attention. I refer to the archetypal dissenter *true* in the Bible: the prophet, who often diverged from the consensus both volubly and vigorously, who challenged the establishment, both religious and civil, and survived. His survival was due to the fact that, in Israel, the right of the prophet to immunity from coercion was recognized, not always in practice, but certainly in principle. Two passages dealing with prophets help to clarify both the nature and the limitations of this immunity. In Deut. 13:1-5, etc., the limits of dissent are defined. Any would-

be prophet who advocates the worship of other gods—
in violation of the first and basic commandment—is to be
executed forthwith. Such dissent goes beyond acceptable
limits, and cannot be tolerated. In Deut. 18, however, a
different sort of question is considered: how to distinguish
between true and false prophets. The basis for the decision
in this case is the validity of their predictions. The prophet
whose predictions are confirmed by events is true; the
prophet whose predictions fail of fulfillment is false. The
story of the confrontation between Jeremiah and Hana-
niah (cf. Jer. 28) illustrates this principle. The point is
that nothing further is said about dealing with the false
prophet, except that his words may be disregarded with
impunity. It is clear that the nature of the test, waiting
until historical events catch up with the predictions, guarantees both men immunity from coercion, at least until
the time limit is exhausted. Thus there was a range of
dissent permitted to prophets, whether true or false. When
Jeremiah was arrested in the Temple and charged with
religious crimes punishable by death, the defense that
proved effective in saving his life was that his words were
in the authentic prophetic tradition, that they conformed
to the pattern established by earlier prophets like Micah,
and thus were considered permissible. It could not then
be determined whether Jeremiah was a true prophet, that
is, whether his words would be confirmed by events. But
on the basis of precedent and permitted dissent, his life
was spared and he continued to prophesy.

We can detect a similar pattern in the career of Jesus.
In his role as prophet, he enjoyed a certain immunity from
coercion, though he vigorously challenged the religious
establishment. It is a sufficient index of the latitude allowed

to religious dissent that his enemies finally had to trump up civil charges against him in order to have him executed. Only Stephen among the early disciples was executed on religious grounds, but this was hardly a dispassionate juridical action; rather it was the violent reaction of a mob egged on by his foes. The executions of John the Baptist and James the Apostle are somewhat different, since they were the victims of the arbitrary judgments of vengeful kings. There is a parallel in the death of Uriah the prophet at the hands of Jehoiakim, the king of Judah, an extraordinary action that shocked the writer, and was contrary to established principle.

Altogether the Biblical record on the fate of prophets is a good one: some were restrained, others were persecuted, and, doubtless, a few were executed. But the many survived to uphold the principle of dissent, and to leave to us, the community of faith, an invaluable legacy of religious freedom.

In any discussion of religious freedom, the Biblical data is important, especially that of the Old Testament, which provides a wide variety of pertinent materials in a vast panorama of human experience. In spite of certain obvious and emphatic statements about religious exclusivity and uniformity, and in spite of the close linkage of religious to civil authority and the application of coercive power to maintain religious unity and conformity, the Bible nevertheless bears eloquent witness to the principle of religious freedom.

In summary, the religious community had a basic right to order its life in accordance with its faith, free from coercion by a foreign power or the civil authorities. Such freedom was guaranteed not only to the holy community of Israel, but to many others as well, whether independent nations or autonomous units in a great empire. Needless to say, the right to immunity from external coercion did not depend upon the truth or validity of the religion professed.

The individual or group within the religious community had a certain, more limited, freedom to dissent from the prevailing pattern of faith and practice. The Bible guarantees to the prophet, the prototype of the dissenter, the right to challenge the establishment, whether civil or religious, without losing either his status or freedom in the community, in principle at least, if not always in practice. And in practice at least, if not necessarily in principle, a false prophet enjoyed the same immunity as the true prophet. In fact, false prophets seemed to have suffered less at the hands of their countrymen than true ones.

The churches and the nations might have spared themselves some of the more tragic episodes in human history had they studied more carefully the Biblical record on religious freedom, and taken its lessons to heart. There may still be value in reviewing the available material.

The Freedom of the Christian

JOHN L. MCKENZIE, S.J.

I AM one of those who is old enough to remember when a declaration of religious liberty seemed as unlikely from the Roman Catholic Church as the canonization of Martin Luther. But the declaration has been made, and more than that, it has been made with no great disturbance and by the vote of an overwhelming majority of the bishops. The Church did not depart as much from an established pattern as we thought, for the pattern really never was established. What we heard was a noisy and persistent minority who knew what they believed. The great majority remained silent, either from fear or from the lack of a clear understanding of their own belief. The Church discovered no new principles in arriving at the Declaration on Religious Liberty, nor did she abandon any old principles. The Church simply reconsidered her identity and mission, and once having recognized herself, she could

have arrived at no other conclusion. That the Church ever
failed to state the principle of religious liberty firmly—
and she did fail—was due to a loss of identity. Deeply
engaged in politics, the Church could not recognize herself, and her decision became partly or even entirely
political.

My task is to discuss the decree against its Biblical background. If I were to limit myself to the explicit discussion
of the New Testament and to the texts quoted, particularly in article 11, my treatment might be thought not
altogether sympathetic with the decree. A fuller and better
selection of texts could have been made and I could pro-
duce a very dull paper by listing the texts I think should
have been used, adding a brief comment to each. This part
of the decree is disappointing because it can leave many
with the impression that this handful of texts is the Biblical
background of the decree. It seems that it will be more
profitable and, I hope, more interesting to the reader to
attempt to state some of the Biblical themes on which
the decree reposes.

The central idea of the decree is the dignity of the
human person. Personal dignity demands that the person
be permitted to realize his personal fulfillment. He can do
this only by exercising his power of responsible decision.
The notion of personal dignity can be viewed philosophically, and, if it is so explained, a very convincing statement
can be produced. Once the nature of the person is understood, it becomes obvious that only the person can make
himself fully what he has the potential to become. He
must do this in society, of course, but society exists in
order that persons may reach their full development

within it. I do no more than notice the philosophical presentation, because it is not my task to expound it or to
criticize it. I do no more than notice that historic man
has rarely been aware of the dignity of the human person.
Historic man has almost always considered that some
human beings are more persons than others, or that some
human beings are ends and other human beings are means.
Historically, human societies have rarely been principles of
freedom. This does not imply that the philosophical presentation is invalid; it suggests that a consideration of the
nature of man does not always coincide with a consideration of the history of man.

We approach the dignity of the human person via the
New Testament, not because the Old Testament has
nothing to say, but because the full dignity of the person
as a religious subject does not emerge in the Old Testament. In the New Testament all Christians become one
in Christ, so that differences of race, social status, and sex
cease to be meaningful. Baptism gives all men freedom in
Christ. This is not specifically religious freedom in the
modern sense of the word. Rather it is freedom from sin
and concupiscence, it is freedom from slavery to the
world. There is a sense in which the Christian freedom of
Paul is very close to the Stoic freedom of the wise man.
The difference, however, is seen when the basis of the two
freedoms are viewed more profoundly. For the Stoic, the
wise man liberates himself. The Christian has been lib-
erated by God through Christ, and the freedom of the
Christian is the freedom to act as a religious subject. No
member of the Church has more or less of this freedom
than another member, for this would mean that some

members are more baptized than others. And since it is God who bestows this freedom, it is not for man to take it away.

It is worth stressing the fact that Christian freedom and Christian equality go together. Any conception of the inequality of persons destroys freedom—if not at once, then in the course of a very short time. Unless we are speaking of equality, we are not speaking of persons; we are speaking of persons with something added—of persons as Jews, Greeks, Scythians, or women, to draw an example from a Christian writer so remote in time that no contemporary allusion can be suspected. We can fill in the more contemporary names and titles for ourselves. These are the factors that Paul says make no distinction between Christians; these would destroy the unity of Christ. What he says fits quite well with the saying of Jesus that those who are officers of his community should become the slaves and lackeys of others. Where inequality might creep in, we have a specific recommendation that it should be compensated. For the Christian can achieve a distinction from other persons only by taking something away from them and what he takes away might turn out to be their power of responsible decision, the only means they have of achieving fulfillment as persons. The dignity of the person is invested with a new sacredness, for the person is a member of Christ and a son of God. Thus it is God's freedom that is attacked when human freedom is attacked. For God has a fulfillment in each person that cannot be achieved through other persons.

This freedom, I said, is freedom to act as a religious subject. This ought to have been explained in more detail and in New Testament terms. The decree speaks of *faith* as the religious commitment, and emphasizes that faith is a personal commitment. But the decree makes the point that no one believes except by his personal decision, and it accepts the principle that compulsion is alien to the genius of the New Testament. When we say, as we so often do, that faith is a gift, we must not forget that the gift carries no compulsion to receive it. I think that the decree would have been stronger, and the notion of compulsion as being alien more plausible, if more consideration had been given to the Christian fulfillment, which is not faith but love. When James said that faith without works is dead, he meant, as we can see clearly in the context, the works of love. Now love, by its nature—here we can appeal to the philosophical consideration—is the height of personal freedom and personal decision, personal commitment and engagement. That love can be compelled is an absurdity; if it were compelled it would not be love. Of course, this is true of love on the merely human level, but what is given to the Christian is love on the divine level. The Christian loves his neighbor not because of his lovable qualities but simply because the neighbor is there. The Christian is to exhibit the sovereign love of God, which is free from all compulsion and free of any particular attraction; therefore, it can be given to all equally, and no one can be excluded from its scope. This is the supreme religious act of the Christian, and he cannot perform it unless he does it with supreme freedom. He must engage himself; no one else can do it on his behalf.

The concrete ideal of Christian love is Jesus himself, who did not employ coercion. The decree refers to those passages of the Gospels in which coercion is explicitly rejected. Jesus employs persuasion and demonstration, but

he does not employ physical or moral force. In the crisis
of his life he met coercion with nonresistance, and thus
he achieved the saving act. Why should Christians ever
have thought that the character of the saving act had
changed? If the Church is the enduring presence of Christ
in the world, should not her share in the saving act manifest the same qualities as the saving act of him whose name
the Church bears? It is shocking to think of the Church
as continuing the role of the Sanhedrin and Pilate in the
passion rather than the role of Jesus. I said that the
Church has not always clearly recognized her identity,
and this is what I meant. At times her leaders have appealed to means of fulfilling her mission that Jesus refused.
No one doubts that this was a demonstration of his sovereign freedom, a freedom that is communicated to his
members.

Love is fulfilled in the works of love, and the New
Testament in more than one context states what some of
the works of love are. I find it piquant that the New
Testament is most explicit about the works of love just
where more recent Christian moralists have insisted that
these works are optional. (I mean such things as nonresistance and the total donation of one's goods to the poor.)
More recent moralists may place greater emphasis on
these acts than the Gospel does, but their position clearly
makes these works of love a matter of personal decision.
The principle of love must be worked out in detail by
each Christian in a manner suitable to his own situation
and his own resources, for ultimately no one except the
person who loves knows whether his love is genuine and
full. It is not for another to impose a ceiling upon his love.
Nor is it for another to teach how to love, since love is

an action that cannot be taught as history and geometry are taught. It is communicated by love received, by love shown in example, by immersion in an atmosphere of love, which ought to be the atmosphere of the Christian community.

This thought leads into another consideration that I have treated elsewhere, and I must beg pardon for being repetitious. I am aware that the consideration is controversial even among interpreters of the Bible, but the proposition is important enough to be set forth once more, especially since it is still open to discussion. The proposition, based on the Gospels and the Epistles of Paul, is that Christianity confers freedom from law. I interpret this proposition to mean that Christianity does not impose obligation on its members. It is clear in St. Paul, and scarcely less clear in the Gospels, that the law of Judaism is annulled for Christians. No distinction is made between various laws or types of law in this annulment. We do not keep a few and throw away the others. Of the 613 precepts that the rabbis counted in the five books of Moses, Jesus retained only two—the love of God above all things and the love of the neighbor as oneself. Paul wrote that he who loves his neighbor has fulfilled the law. And Christian interpreters have never contended that the law of Judaism remained valid, even when they have been uncertain about some of its contents.

That the annulment of obligation is a consequence of the annulment of the law I deduce from the fact that no other law is substituted for the law of Judaism. The Christian will do the acts of love from the motivation of love or they are not Christian acts. We may put it this way: the Christian who does not commit adultery from a motive of obligation has done nothing wrong, but he has done nothing good in the Christian sense. He has not risen above the morality of the law, and he has not made his righteousness more abundant than the righteousness of the scribes and Pharisees. If one thinks of morality as comprised in love instead of law, it is extremely difficult to define a point at which one has done all that one ought. Love is not considered in terms of what one ought to do.

It is a real question whether we have ever shown full confidence in the freedom and responsibility implied in the morality of love, and therefore whether we have allowed Christian personal dignity to reach that fullness that lies within its power. It seems undeniable that Jesus released the power of love as an adequate principle of an entirely new set of human relations. Christians who are endowed with the Spirit have the capacity to execute the commandment of love by their personal decisions. Some will never reach it, others will fail to reach its fullness, and all will fail at times to reach even its minimum level. Jesus seems to have preferred these risks to other risks, risks involved in the principle of obligation. Certainly these other risks include the preservation of the principle of pharisaism, and the risk of creating a class of Christian scribes. They include the risk of reducing the ideal of love to a controllable minimal level of obligation that can be imposed. These risks we have run, and I will not go into the consequences.

The New Testament speaks of freedom of the Christian; the decree on freedom speaks of the religious freedom of all men. How is the Biblical base of freedom extended to those who are not members of the Christian community? Here it might seem both wiser and safer to rest the principle on philosophical reasoning. I am not sure that the philosophical basis of freedom is more meaningful here than elsewhere. For Christian freedom does touch the freedom of others very deeply, and for the Christian this is ultimately the factor that will mean most to him. In its simplest terms, Christian freedom means that other men must have the freedom to become Christians. If they do not become Christians by a free personal decision, they do not become Christians at all. They cannot be compelled into the way of freedom, for it would cease to be the way of freedom if they were.

However, historically, Christianity has often shown little confidence in the power of the Gospel, preferring to strengthen the Gospel by various types of pressure. Christians have shunned the encounter with the world, the free encounter of the market place. Had they deep faith in that which they profess, they would fear an encounter with no one, confident that the power and truth of the *satyagraha* Gospel is greater than all human arguments and all human force. Yet it is precisely these means, arguments and force, that have sometimes been employed to propagate Christianity or to maintain it. Although the unbeliever is quite safe from an authentic Christian, it is not difficult to understand why he is apprehensive when he is confronted with any other kind. It is the other kind that makes this decree necessary and valuable. The declaration does not create any more authentic Christians, but it at least keeps any other kind from being the spokesmen of the Church.

Ultimately the assurance of freedom of religion for all men rests on the conviction of the Christian community. I am aware that this may appear to some to be a foundation less stout than they could wish, but what is to substi-

tute for this Christian conviction? The conciliar decree is
a beginning and not an end. It should help Christians,
and in particular Roman Catholic Christians for whom it
speaks, to understand that religious freedom for all men
is not a matter of tolerance or concession or compromise
with a lesser evil. It is an act of virtue, an act of Christian
love, and an act of apostolic zeal. It guarantees the Gospel
against corruption. And I spare you the obvious comments on how it might make Christianity a little more
attractive. I do not think it is in our power to make Christianity attractive, but it is unfortunately within our power
to make it repulsive.

There is a final aspect of the decree that does not really
fall within the scope of the decree. The topic pertains to
and is opened in the constitution of the Church. That it
is opened will permit further discussion, for the topic has
been discussed extensively in recent years. This aspect is
religious freedom within the Church as well as outside
it. I hesitate to add this consideration, because it may
appear irrelevant, and may even be thought a hobby-
horse that I brought along because I have a chance for
another ride. But I think it is pertinent, and I shall try to
explain why. Perhaps a simple, if incomplete, way to say
it is that freedom is of one piece; either you believe in it
or you do not. It has been my effort here to set forth the
Biblical basis of religious freedom. Examination shows
that it is Christian freedom within the Church that best
guarantees, at least for Christians, freedom of other religions. The Church can be no more convinced of the right
of freedom of those who are not her members than she
is convinced of the right of freedom of those who are her
members. The history of the failure of the Church to

speak clearly on religious freedom is accompanied by a
history of her failure to accord her members that personal
dignity and power of decision that is theirs as Christians.
This history is so long and so complex that we now find
ourselves in the position of reaching for something we
are not sure we want and defending something we are
not sure we like. Let no one be apprehensive about
demands for excessive freedom. For what it is worth, my
experience is that most Catholics are afraid of freedom and
do not even want as much as they have. And because they
are afraid of it for themselves, they are afraid of it for
others. No doubt this attitude is changing in what is called
"the new breed," and it would be interesting to be around
long enough to see how "new" the new breed is in 1986.
But at present it is still true, as it has been for a long
time, that practically no important decisions in the Church
are made by any one under forty, and very few by any
one under fifty. The change in attitude may be coming,
but it is not just around the corner.

In evading freedom Catholics evade responsibility. They
permit the character of their Christian fulfillment to be
determined by another. Where they ought to look for
leadership they look for control, and it must be said that
they have little trouble in finding it. By doing so they
renounce the freedom to act as a religious subject. This
can be ultimately the renunciation of Christian love. I
am optimistic enough to think that discontent with this
type of managed Christianity will grow, and that more
and more people will see that they will be as free as they
insist on being. To some of us older and more timorous
churchmen, it will look as if the whole structure is totter-
ing; but that is because our perspective is from the past.

We are, I think, on the eve of some important structural changes. These changes can put Christian fulfillment within a nearer reach of Catholics than is now possible. These changes can be conducted in an orderly fashion, for the Church has the resources to grow without the mess of a revolution. But she will grow, and those who attempt to stop history will have the difficulties usually experienced by those who attempt it. Recently I have been going over the Epistles to the Corinthians. It is simply impossible to imagine a church of this type today. But if the Christians of Corinth were really able to move where Paul led them, we have little reason to think we are better than they because we are more organized. The Church can survive the disorder of development better than she can stand the living death of organized immobility. We have not yet seen that the Declaration on Religious Freedom has profound implications within the life of the Church as well as in her posture toward the world. With the declaration the Church has disclosed her true identity, and it will be impossible to conceal it in the future.

beautiful!

PART IV

THE CONCILIAR DOCUMENT
AND AMERICAN LIFE

The Conciliar Document:
A Politico-Legal Excursus

VICTOR G. ROSENBLUM

I GREW up in a neighborhood in New York, up in the Bronx, where we were never inclined or allowed to worry about whether we were free to worship as we believed. It was a neighborhood that consisted of about 48 per cent Jews and 48 per cent Catholics, and the only problem that we ever had was in deciding how we Jews and Catholics, who were the establishment, were going to run things so that we would be nice to the poor WASP minority. We never were taught that we were any kind of minority with problems impinging upon our freedom of worship. My initial notions about ecumenism were probably based on the Saturday night poker games in which the Farrell's, Whelan's, and O'Neill's joined the Rosenblum's, Levin's, and Levy's for great evenings of argumentation, debate, and card-dealing. In a subjective sense, then, I feel un-qualified to comment with any degree of incisiveness upon the Declaration on Religious Freedom. Whatever the doctrinal transition may have been in the stance of the Church, my own upbringing was within an environment of friendly, at times boisterous, congeniality. Whether bargains were better at the bazaars at Our Lady of Angels or at the Kingsbridge Heights Jewish Center hardly seemed a basis for threatening my inbred belief in religious freedom.

I set this subjective data before you at the outset because I am not at all certain that even the aspirations of a political scientist or lawyer are adequate in light of this background to provide the critical analysis that this institute warrants. Nonetheless, with sheer bravado substituting for background, I would like to observe that there are at least three major kinds of significance to the conciliar document: theological, legal, and political. The theological has been dealt with earlier, for which I am most grateful. As a legal document, its significance will depend for internal impact on the interpretation accorded it by the Church. But it has what we might well term a politico-legal status as well. I have used the hybrid term, "politico-legal," because the document is important both as an instrument of policy innovation and as a source of guidelines or norms for human conduct, which will be subject to administration and enforcement by the Church. When I use the term "political," I use it not as a mode of invidious comparison or of denigration, but with the fullest zest and zeal that political scientists can bring to the analysis of their favorite subject.

The conciliar document is a brilliant politico-legal document in much the same way that the Constitution of the United States was a work of brilliance. It is sufficiently

explicit to make ringingly clear the fact that men are not
to be treated unequally because of the diversity of their
religious preferences. At the same time, there is sufficient
ambiguity in the document to allow for growth through
interpretation and administration, which is essential to the
document's long-range sustenance. Guidelines are often
preferable to orders, and far from fearing all amorphous
or ambiguous declarations, I feel that many encourage subsequent generations of policy-makers to accept the mantle
of responsibility to improve on the work of their
predecessors.

The trouble, from my vantage point, with 100 per cent
meticulousness and explicitness in 100 per cent of a document is that it may detract from the role that is to be
played by the interpreters and administrators. Indifference
to the administration of even the soundest document is
infinitely worse, in my book, than compassion, breadth,
and understanding in the administration of even the most
nebulous guideline.

I applaud the conciliar document's specificity with
regard to man's inherent right not to be coerced in his
religious beliefs. The failure to spell out the particular
criteria for invocation and evaluation of man's choices is
not a defect, for such explicitness in every detail could
bind unnecessarily and irrevocably those who will be
charged with its interpretation.

Nonetheless, I do feel that there are several aspects of
the document, as a legal document, that pose dilemmas
from the standpoint of legal construction in that they offer
what Robert Carr once referred to as "dual thorough-
fares" for interpretation. I would like to cite some of the
text from the declaration, using as my source the pamphlet

edition published by the National Catholic Welfare Conference. For example, insofar as the American constitutional system is concerned, I find that the statement on aid to religion poses a question about the consistency of the document with the prevalent legal stance of our society.

In the last paragraph of article 3, it states: "The religious acts whereby men, in private and in public and out of a sense of personal conviction, direct their lives to God transcend by their very nature the order of terrestrial and temporal affairs. Government therefore ought indeed to take account of the religious life of the citizenry and show it favor, since the function of Government is to make provision for the common welfare." I do not presume to know the full implications of the term "show it favor"; time will have to develop its meaning. If by "show it favor," however, the text means provide governmental support, then does that, in turn, require providing governmental support equally to all religions presently within the society? Or does it require provision of governmental support for certain religions and not for others? If it means providing any kind of direct support at all to any religious group, what has happened to our traditional concern about the dangers that governmental support may well imply governmental control?

A second point I would like to consider concerns the relationship between the document as a declaration and the document as a set of legal requirements for Catholics. There is majestic and inspiring language throughout the declaration, but how shall it be administered and enforced? I found that such points as the second, third, and fourth had vast emotional appeal to me. The point made, for example, in the third paragraph of article 3 says that, "On his part, man perceives and acknowledges the imperatives of the divine law through the mediation of conscience. In all his activity a man is bound to follow his conscience in order that he may come to God, the end and purpose of life. It follow that he is not to be forced to act in a manner contrary to his conscience." I find in this the fullest nobility of prose.

I believe also that the language regarding the rights of religious communities not to be hindered either by legal measures or by administrative action on the part of government in the selection, training, appointment, and transferral of their own ministers, in communicating with religious authorities abroad, and erecting buildings for religious purposes, and in the acquisition and use of suitable funds or properties, to be vital to my own conception of pluralism in American society.

Equally admirable is the language in article 2 dealing with immunity from coercion. It stresses the need not only for immunity from overt instrumentalities of coercion but for psychological freedom of the individual as well: "However, men cannot discharge these obligations in a manner in keeping with their own nature unless they enjoy immunity from external coercion as well as psychological freedom."

Accepting the majesty and beauty of the language does not resolve the problem of what follows from the words. What requirements does the language impose? Viewing the declaration as a lawyer might look at a legal document, one notes that in one part the declaration urges, in another part it exhorts, and in still another it talks about the specific duties incumbent upon the teacher. Are the urgings, exhortations, and recitals of duties separate or are they related, one to the other? The language on urging is contained in article 8. It says: "Wherefore this Vatican Council urges everyone, especially those who are charged with the task of educating others, to do their utmost to form men who, on the one hand, will respect the moral order and be obedient to lawful authority, and, on the other hand, will be lovers of true freedom—men, in other words, who will come to decisions on their own judgment and in the light of truth, govern their activities with a sense of responsibility, and strive after what is true and right, willing always to join with others in cooperative effort." That is an urge to all. The language of article 15 states: "The Council exhorts Catholics, and it directs a plea to all men, most carefully to consider how greatly necessary religious freedom is, especially in the present condition of the human family." Now, does the language of urging in article 8 and the language of exhortation in article 15 make the majestic declarations I had quoted earlier the equivalents only of legal dicta, or do they place on the shoulders of mankind, and especially on Catholics, responsibilities in addition to those cited earlier?

The language in article 14 with regard to the responsibility of the teacher neither urges nor exhorts. It speaks of duty. In the second paragraph of article 14, the declaration states: "The church is, by the will of Christ, the teacher of the truth. It is her duty to give utterance to, and authoritatively to teach, that truth which is Christ Himself, and also to declare and confirm by her authority those principles of the moral order which have their origin in human nature itself. Furthermore, let Christians walk in wisdom in the face of those outside, 'in the Holy Spirit, in unaffected love, in the word of truth,' and let them be

about their task of spreading the light of life with all confidence and apostolic courage, even to the shedding of
their blood."

Does the provision regarding apostolic courage, even to
the shedding of blood, apply only to the teaching of the
Church's doctrines, or does it apply to all other points
that are contained in the document as well? Does it mean,
as I hope it would, that the duty to support all of what is
contained in the document about man's dignity and freedom from coercion and the pursuit of his conscience
should not only be *considered* but should be *taught* as
part of the doctrine of the Church and maintained with
the apostolic courage mentioned in article 14? Is this the
meaning and intent of the language in article 6 which
appears to establish residuary responsibility that carries
over to the entire document? Article 6 says: "Therefore
the care of the right to religious freedom devolves upon
the whole citizenry, upon social groups, upon government,
and upon the Church and other religious communities, in
virtue of the duty of all toward the common welfare, and
in the manner proper to each." The claim that article 6
permeates the declaration and that the requirement of
apostolic courage runs through the entire document would
be stronger legally if it had been reaffirmed in the last section. If the most forceful language of *duty* were utilized
at the very end of the document, it might have made it
clearer, to the layman at least, that there is an all-permeat-
ing duty to teach all of what is contained within the document, and not merely to consider the nobler language
cited while teaching only in the more limited and traditional areas of Catholic doctrine.

I have striven to find something to cavil about in the

document from the vantage point of the layman concerned with the document's implementation. Clearly, the
document is, without any question, an espousal of pluralism. It supports the ideals and aspirations of constitutional
government and democracy. Yet, while recognizing this,
we are all sufficiently sophisticated to know that language
alone neither accounts for nor constitutes all of man's
behavior. Will our society be enriched as a consequence
of human behavior in response to the document, or will
the document meet with what social scientists have termed
anomie or apathy, and will it, consequently, atrophy in
practice?

I don't think that any of us in the lay community knows
the answer to that one. All that is clear on this matter is
that the traditional anti-Catholic has to go looking for a
new dogma. Those who, in an earlier period, saw the
Church as a monolithic entity, commanding the most
minute and mundane responses of her adherents, must
surely be frustrated in evaluating the impact of the document. If they continue to believe in the automatic obedience of every Catholic to every official declaration, then
they must obviously believe in spontaneous compliance
and will have to hail the instant pluralism made feasible,
if not mandatory, by the Church's doctrine declared in
the schema. If, on the other hand, they must concede that
instant and total compliance is not feasible, then they must
also acknowledge that the Church is not the autocratic
monolith they had conjured and cherished, and they must
now confess error, if nothing else.

Illusions, prejudices, and presuppositions about the
Church must be re-examined, and many of them will be

punctured. There are, of course, many kinds of dangerous illusions. I wonder if, when the document deals with some aspects of lay society, there may not be something of an illusion *by* rather than *about* the Church. I refer to article 7, and I would be grateful for enlightenment on whether that is an illusion about the role of juridical norms in our society. The statement says: "However, government is not to act in an arbitrary fashion or in an unfair spirit of partisanship. Its action is to be controlled by juridical norms which are in conformity with the objective moral order." I am happy to find the additional language of "norms which are in conformity with the objective moral order," for I think it is important for us to bear in mind that the line of decision-making that has been pursued in recent years by the United States Supreme Court is by no means a line of decision-making that has been or is likely to be perpetual within our society. It is important to bear in mind that even our courts were capable, in an earlier era, of developing juridical norms that provided a juridical base for man's inequality and for man's inhumanity to his fellow man.

It does not require too deep a sojourn into history to recall that in 1857 it was the Supreme Court of the United States, in the infamous case of Dred Scott versus Sanford, that declared unconstitutional the last-ditch effort on the part of the United States Congress to prevent the coming holocaust. It said, gratuitously and evilly, that the man in whose name the suit was brought was not entitled to have the action adjudicated because the Fifth Amendment to the Constitution of the United States could be invoked only by *persons*. The due process clause of the Fifth

Amendment, said the Supreme Court at that time, applied
to persons and Dred Scott was not a person since, as a
slave, he was merely an article of property.

If the decision in the Dred Scott case were a purely isolated decision, one could perhaps say that any institution
is capable of an occasional aberration. But much of that
entire era in the history of the United States Supreme
Court was permeated by a set of values utterly antithet-
ical to our belief in the equality of all mankind. One finds
even in the post-Civil War period a series of decisions on
the part of the Supreme Court striking down as unconstitutional effort after effort made by the United States
Congress and made by the states to try to resolve the evils
of man's inhumanity and to set the nation on a course of
equality. When Congress, after the Civil War, passed a
series of civil rights statutes, it was the Supreme Court
of the United States, in a series of cases highlighted by
the civil rights cases of 1883, that struck down many of
those provisions on the ground that it was not the business
of Congress to seek to establish human equality. Under
the Fourteenth Amendment, Congress, according to the
Supreme Court, could act only to counteract actions for
which the states alone had been responsible.

The Supreme Court also struck down as unconstitutional
the efforts of reconstruction governments in states like
Louisiana to outlaw segregation. The Supreme Court had
no hesitation to invoke whatever concept of the Constitution seemed available to do this. When the State of Louisiana passed a law prohibiting racial segregation in any
public facility, the Supreme Court struck this down as
unconstitutional on the ground that it interfered with
interstate commerce. But when the State of Mississippi

passed a statute requiring racial regregation on all modes of public transportation, the Supreme Court of the United States upheld the constitutionality of that statute and said that this was not an interference with interstate commerce because the State Supreme Court had said it was not.

I cite this dark period in American juridical history so that we will be aware of the fact that juridical norms need not perennially follow in the direction in which they appear to be moving in other parts of society. It is just as possible for the judiciary to move backward as it is to move forward. Hence I would suggest that there be no more absolute faith placed in lay juridical norms, per se, than is placed in any other single institution.

It appears to me, then, that what is most important about the declaration is not that it provides us with definitive answers. Definitive answers need not, and perhaps even should not, be given at this time. The value of the document, from my vantage point, is that it opens the doors for discussion, for communication, for analysis, and for continuous negotiation and dialogue.

These, indeed, are the finest manifestations of man's rationality. The very process of sincere exchange of diverse views strengthens the dedication of all of us to learning, to understanding, and to affirmation and enhancement of man's integrity, conscience, and reason. The open door and the open mind, which receives and examines alternative views and contentions, are essential to the quest for and the fulfillment of justice. In that respect, the gracious invitation and hospitality of the Bellarmine Institute are to me as much indicators of the commitment to freedom as the eloquence of the document itself.

The Conciliar Declaration
and the American Declaration

PHILIP S. DENENFELD

IF I were a Catholic or a theologian, I am sure my perspective would be so different that I would view and respond to this statement as historically significant and reflective of remarkable change. Since I am neither, my strongest impression of the conciliar Declaration on Religious Freedom is of its contradictory characteristics, as though it could not quite make up its mind. It seems to me to resemble in many of its key assertions a treasured domestic document that predates it by nearly two centuries, the Bill of Rights. Yet many of its basic assumptions work at cross-purposes with that statement of our national liberties, for its primary commitment, I think, is to religion, not to freedom. In the conciliar document freedom becomes a means to an end, a sectarian end. It is endorsed as a human right, but tied to the conviction that its proper use will lead to a predetermined religious truth. Given its source, this is hardly surprising, and I am not complaining about that. It is just that the fact diminishes my enthusiasm generated by its many qualities that please me, and causes me concern about the impact of this statement on American life and attitudes.

I recall thinking to my self as I read the first few pages of the declaration that the deletion of a few of the partisan references—which somehow seemed incongruous—would leave an appropriate introduction to the Bill of Rights: "the dignity of the human person," "constitutional limits should be set to the powers of government, in order that there may be no encroachment on the rightful freedom of the person and of associations," "the quest for the values proper to the human spirit," "all men are to be immune from coercion on the part of individuals or of social groups." This is in the spirit of Madison and Jefferson, who long ago convinced me that they had provided sound, durable, ingenious answers for the problems of religious freedom in a diverse society.

Somewhere along the line, though, I got uneasy. I think it was when I came to a familiar old argument, familiar because I have disputed it for years with friends in CEF, that government must provide a "genuinely free choice of schools and of other means of education . . . without imposing unjust burdens on parents." Then I began to have the feeling that I had been there before. My civil libertarian instincts now aroused, I lowered my sights from the universal perspective demanded by a Vatican Council statement to focus on a comfortable homebred church-state fight. This reaction may mark me as dreadfully provincial, but I think it has some legitimacy, particularly as

I was asked to respond personally to this declaration as I saw it to apply to American life.

I read back through the first five pages and noted again those phrases that had struck me as incongrous: "religious freedom . . . which men demand as necessary to fulfill their duty to worship God," "a moral obligation to speak the truth, especially religious truth," "In all his activity a man is bound to follow his conscience in order that he may come to God, the end and purpose of life." Perfectly proper statements for a Vatican Council to make—their absence, in fact, would be remarkable—and undoubtedly reflective of the beliefs of millions of Americans. But when they become the basis of a philosophy that in turn dictates a definition of the proper relationship between church and state for a whole nation, they are no longer a distracting admixture with Madison and Jefferson; they are contradictions that violate the spirit of the Bill of Rights. They lead to conclusions that many men have reached, and should be free to believe and propagate, but they are quite different assumptions from those that underlie the national philosophy of religious liberty expressed in the First Amendment. It is the conflict with what I believe to be this national philosophy, embodied in our laws and in our social fabric, that disturbs me most about the Declaration on Religious Freedom.

A fundamental assumption of the conciliar declaration that poses this basic conflict—and which makes this declaration, for me, a commitment to religion rather than to freedom—is the traditional view that men's private and public religious acts, directing their lives to God, "transcend by their very nature the order of terrestrial and temporal affairs." This is an obvious premise of many religions, a primary source of their strength and attractiveness. But it is not a universal view, and, more important, it is not necessarily a sufficient premise from which to evolve a definition of a sound relationship between government and religion. It has never been sufficient in America to sustain officially the logical consequence stated by the declaration that "Government therefore ought indeed to take account of the religious life of the citizenry and *show it favor*, since the function of government is to make provision for the common welfare" (emphasis added). We have as a nation shown it favor, but not of the sort called for here and not because of any national commitment to religion. The cumulative and evolving interpretation of the First Amendment to the Constitution, our national statement of the pinciple of religious freedom, makes clear that we respect the *right* of a citizen to accept, or reject, the transcendancy of religious acts. This is quite a different matter. For one thing, it has led us not into theocracy or into an official religion, but into a nation of more than 250 religions, plus millions of nonbelievers and doubters. And all of these religions and people have a guaranteed roughly equal standing before the law and the government, if not in the hearts of their countrymen.

At this point it may be necessary for me to state that I am not criticizing the Vatican Council declaration for failing to do what it never intended to do, agree with the Bill of Rights. It is, after all, a statement of one faith, not all, and directed to an entire world, not a single nation. My concern, rather, is that its impact on American life, Catholic and non-Catholic, could be divisive because of what I think is its basic contradiction of our concept of religious freedom. Both the purposes and many of the assumptions of the declaration seem to me so different from the rationale of the Constitution and the Bill of Rights that even when these documents seem to agree with each other, and to employ almost identical language, they are actually in conflict. The two conflicting frames of reference permit the illusion of sameness, but prevent true agreement.

For example, when the Council declares "that no one is to be forced to act in a manner contrary to his own beliefs, nor is anyone to be restrained from acting in accordance with his own beliefs," it has the ring of American freedom, but this soon fades into "the right to this immunity continues to exist *even in those who do not live up to their obligation of seeking the truth and adhering to it. . . .*" (my emphasis). This is a different world, one with prescribed truths and the moral obligation to seek them, with toleration for those who have not found them or do not choose to seek them. It is, I think, the peculiar virtue and strength of our concept of religious liberty that we make no such prescriptions or distinctions, and that we forbid our government to do so. And it is this conception that defines the proper role of government in the highly sensitive area of personal belief.

To return to the obligation of government to show favor to the religious life of the citizenry, I think it indisputable that this country has done so from its inception. As a nation we have always recognized that religious belief is sufficiently important to enough of our citizens to deserve the special protection of our government. Tax exemption for recognized religions, with certain qualifications, renders them a favored status as old as the country itself. And the First Amendment was the *first* amendment.

It places religious liberty in the very exalted company of free speech and free press. To that extent, there is no conflict with the conciliar declaration, but the declaration alone misses the whole complexity and intent of our national position. The same First Amendment recognizes the controversial nature of religion and attitudes toward it, and acknowledges the history of religious persecution and bigotry and thus the fact that it *requires* special protection. And further, in prohibiting the government from actively supporting religion, the amendment recognizes the dangers of establishing any partnership or significant involvement between the government and the churches. In Madison's own words, and in the ensuing interpretations of the First Amendment, government is prevented from favoring any or all religions, from favoring one religion over others, or from favoring the religious over the non-religious. We are, of course, still determining the proper application of this philosophy to specific issues, but there is no serious debate about the philosophy. Certainly no recognized authority argues, as does the Council, that the state is obligated to discriminate in behalf of or against religion.

In this context it seems evident that our national view is that an individual or a sectarian institution may believe that the purpose of religious freedom is to fulfill one's duty to God, or that coming to God is the end and purpose of life, or that peace and justice are enhanced by adherence to a particular religious conviction; but that none of these beliefs has the official endorsement of the nation, and that, in fact, we deny any but incidental public support to such persons or institutions in the advancement of their religious views and objectives.

As a nation, I believe, we have not shared the assumption of the conciliar declaration that religious belief, or any particular faith, has singular powers to benefit the individual citizen or the country that would make it so essential to our national welfare as to demand governmental support. Rather, we have recognized that enough of our citizenry desires and may be significantly affected by a free religious choice that the latter ought to be available and must be protected from those who would deny it. Thus we have established a powerful but controlled public mechanism whereby this could be accomplished. It is based on the philosophy that freedom, within reasonable limits, may be used as individuals choose to use it.

In other words, the Constitution does intend to assure the independence of each religion (again, with limits) and to protect it from coercion or control by others or by the government itself, but it does not intend to insure its existence. That decision is up to the people, who may of their own free will support or reject a religion. As I have indicated, the state, legally prohibited from exerting influence on this decision, is the neutral agent of the people, a referee deemed necessary to the existence of a meaningful freedom of choice.

This philosophy neither states nor implies that any unique power of religion should "care for the salvation of men"; it provides, instead, that each man may believe that, and act on his belief, if he so chooses. And it certainly does not mean that government has a prescribed obligation to nurture religious faith or any particular religion; it could hardly mean that while it prohibits government from supporting religion. The churches in America are really intended to operate on a pure form of nonprofit free enterprise, a survival of the fittest, as distasteful as that figure may be. They are one of many competing supplicants for private and public support, each of which claims to satisfy an important need. What the people freely choose in religion—and are willing to support—they shall have, and government sees to it that the rules of the game are observed in the making of that choice. Under those rules religions have come and gone (at the will of the people), every religion has been subjected to attack by someone, most religions have sought in some way at some time to get the neutral referee in their corner, and probably most have been unhappy because neither the government nor a sufficient number of people recognized what they were convinced was the unique contribution their faith could make to the nation. But through it all religion and religious freedom have flourished in this country.

I cannot, of course, explore in this relatively brief presentation many of the implications of the conciliar declaration as applied to American religious freedom, but I would like to examine one statement from the declaration that seems to me to demonstrate the incompatibility of the two frames of reference—the dominance of religion in the declaration and the dominance of freedom in the American Constitution. It appears in article 5: "Parents, moreover, have the right to determine, in accordance with their own religious beliefs, the kind of religious education that their children are to receive. Government, in consequence, must acknowledge the right of parents to make a genuinely free choice of schools and of other means of education, and the use of this freedom of choice is not to be made a reason for imposing unjust burdens on parents, whether directly or indirectly." One will recognize

this position—since its language has already been trans-
lated into practical application in this country—as a highly
contentious one in America today, the heart of a long-
standing and heated church-state controversy. Professor
Rosenblum has cited it briefly as a source of potential constitutional conflict, and earlier Father Canavan observed
that while the passage may have been intended to censure
those Communist countries that forbid the free practice
of religion, it also stands as a censure of American practices in the support of education and educational choice.
My personal response, as I have already stated, was to the
striking similarity between its logic and language and that
of the CEF literature that I have read and discussed for
years with those who maintain just this position, and who
will now cite Vatican authority for their views. Whatever international application the Vatican Council may
have intended, it appears to me that each country may be
expected to read this declaration in its own particular
national context.

I singled out the passage, however, not merely for its
potential for controversy, but for the dramatic fashion in
which it poses the problem of dual perspective. The
rationale of the conciliar statement led the Council quite
naturally into a position on education, and there we need
not speculate, for we can draw on the American
experience.

Throughout the declaration, great and wise emphasis is
laid on the Council's consistent opposition to coercion in
religious decisions and its insistence on the necessity of the
independence of the Church in order to fulfill her divine
mission. Both the rejection of coercion and the support of
the independence of churches are positions in complete

accord with what I believe to be the basis for religious freedom in America. But the implied proposal for government subsidy of churches, the inescapable American meaning embodied in the quoted statement, seems to me a sure way to nullify both.

The key words in the quotation are "must," "genuinely free," and "unjust burden." They derive, I think, from a perspective foreign to our traditional means of protecting religious freedom, and that perspective leads inevitably to coercion and a surrender of independence.

We have, through our courts, acknowledged the right of parents to exert religious influence on their children (though limits have been set to safeguard the children's health and welfare), and we have provided that parents may reject the public school education available to all, regardless of their religious choice, in favor of a religious education that meets general academic standards applied to all schools. This, apparently, still does not constitute a *genuinely* free choice, since the financial burden of such a choice is private, not public, and cannot be borne easily by all who might prefer a religious education. Moreover, this financial obligation is labeled in the declaration as an "unjust" burden. Presumably, in an American context this means that since religious persons must support a public school system, it is "unjust" that they must also pay for a parochial school if they choose to send their children to one.

The answer to this position—and it does not need to be labored—is that Americans of all faiths, or of no faith, accept as citizens the obligation to support a public school system, to which we do have a national commitment. Elderly people, childless couples, and single persons all contribute to this system, though they receive no direct benefit from it—and this is not considered unjust. The schools are available to all and cannot be used to inculcate anyone's religious views, a deficiency that may be remedied by home and church. Though such an arrangement does not always satisfy those who believe that a proper education must rest on a religious foundation, it is the best system yet devised to give a common education without disturbing the delicate balance of our religious liberties.

We have seen compromise attempts to make this system at least partially "just" in the perspective of the conciliar declaration, though I doubt that they would be intended or acceptable solutions. Such a solution would require that every religious view somehow be represented on an equal or proportionate basis in the curriculum of every public school, or that a sectarian curriculum be established by the majority faith in each particular school and imposed on the losers, who, by law, must attend a school. These were among serious alternatives considered and rejected by the Supreme Court in its prayer and Bible-reading decisions.

A stronger possibility, and probably the intention that will be attributed to the Vatican Council, is government subsidization of religious schools, with every parent free to elect public or parochial education. But what then happens to the independence of the churches and the rejection of coercion?

First, briefly, the question of independence. Even if government could ignore the fact that it is constitutionally forbidden to support religion, the churches could not avoid the fact of life that what government subsidizes it controls, in the name of the public whose agent it is.

Government-subsidized religion would be—and should be
—government-controlled religion. It would be accountable
to the general public, which paid for it, and subject to the
same standards, demands, and restrictions imposed on the
public schools. The greater the subsidy, the greater the
dependence. The parochial school would, in time, become
an extension of the public school system, rather than a
meaningful alternative to it. To maintain its independence,
a church, and a religious people, must assume the responsibility for its choices and accept its obligations, or independence is a word without meaning.

As to the impropriety of coercion as a means of achieving religious ends, this is already well recognized in our
present basis for religious liberty. Our religious choices
are free, and they are made in the full light of the obligations that accompany them—spiritual, social, psychological,
and financial. If these demands become unbearable, relief
is not available in an encroachment on the rights of others,
who have also made a free choice. And, ironically, government, potentially the most terrible agent of coercion, is,
in our system, the primary protecting agent against coercive intrusion on the freedom of those choices. If, however, that government were to subsidize religion, using
the only funds available—public tax monies contributed
involuntarily—then, indeed, support of religion would be
achieved by coercion. The neutral referee would become
a powerful collector and distributor of church revenues.
Not only would free religious choice be lost, but also
would a deplorable interfaith competition for public lar-
gesse be on with a vengeance. In some ways it has already
begun. The avoidance of such foreseeable consequences
seems to me far wiser than an empty debate about who is

the coercer and who the coerced. It is such divisive practical consequences as this, flowing from interpretations of a philosophy now apparently endorsed by a Vatican statement, that trouble me about the conciliar declaration.

There is, I believe, a remarkable wisdom, a true genius, in the method this nation has devised, and is continually refining, for maintaining religious freedom in the midst of great diversity. It respects and protects religion and religious choice, but it does so through a commitment to an abstract freedom and a confidence that individuals and institutions will accept the responsibilities and reasonable limitations imposed by that freedom. The declaration of the Vatican Council, though it appears to share the American dedication to religious liberty, seems to differ sufficiently in its fundamental means and purposes to be out of harmony with the genius of the Constitution.

PART V

THE CHALLENGE
OF RELIGIOUS FREEDOM

The Need to Affirm
Religious Freedom

J. V. LANGMEAD CASSERLEY

As has been already pointed out by a previous contributor to this book, the Declaration on Religious Freedom of Vatican Council II, given to us in this seventh decade of the twentieth century, differs rather significantly from the Constitution of the United States and from the treatment of this subject usually accorded to it in the literature of classical Americanism, bequeathed from the last quarter of the eighteenth century. I would begin by agreeing that this difference is undeniable and would observe that it is probably inevitable. I would disagree, however, with those who would suppose that the literature of classical Americanism on this or any other subject is by nature final and irreformable. I have noticed again and again that what we may call the conservative-liberal brand of American thought, which might equally well be described as liberal-conservative, inevitably begins with the eighteenth century. Sad enough, it sometimes seems to end there. For while it is true that this peculiarly gifted century provided its successors with many profound insights, it bequeathed them to us in literary and though forms unduly restrictive and purely parochial in the temporal sense.

The chief difference, for example, between the treatment of the subject of religious liberty in the literature of classical Americanism, on the one hand, and the decree of Vatican Council II, on the other, is that the former is chiefly interested in the right of the nonconforming individual not to be compelled against his will to defer to the rules of any particular religious institution. The interest is chiefly in the danger that one religious institution or church may oppress another, or, at the most, that religious forces may attempt to suppress the proper freedom of the nonreligious man. No doubt that this did seem to be the chief danger of the eighteenth century, but the context of Vatican Council II in the twentieth century is quite a different one. When we discuss this subject today, what chiefly concern us are aggressive attacks on religious belief and conduct by fiercely antireligious governments, as for example, the laicist French governments of the first decade of this century and the regimes created by the Russian and Nazi revolutions. In other words, when Vatican Council II, and indeed all churches in the twentieth century, discuss the subject of religious liberty, they are not talking about the liberty of men to be irreligious if they choose, but rather the liberty of men to be religious and conform to the practices of the churches in which they firmly believe. We must always be careful to distinguish between irreligious liberty and religious liberty, for irreligious liberty can easily be conferred by an irreligious government without granting any genuine religious liberty at all. For example, in contemporary Russia the theory is that the irreligious man has complete liberty to propagate his unbelief, whereas the religious man is free to do no more than worship.

But whereas it is quite possible to grant irreligious liberty and withhold religious liberty, we have learned in the twentieth century, and the fathers of Vatican Council II have learned it too, that it is not possible to secure religious liberty without granting irreligious liberty, whereas irreligious liberty does not appear either to imply or to demand total religious liberty. If all that is required is to secure the right of men not to belong to a church or conform to its practices, it is quite unnecessary to declare that those who do wish to belong to a church must have the right to do so. Because the declaration is so much more relevant to our historical context, it seems to me that the Vatican Council decree is in many ways superior, more productive, more fruitful, and more profound than most of the conventional notions and formulations about religious liberty that we have inherited from the eighteenth-century Enlightenment.

I am a philosophical theologian and not very fond of exegesis, so that my commentary on the Council's decree will read between the lines rather than along them. The mere exegete can hardly avoid some species of fundamentalism. The same thing is true in our schools of law as well as in our schools of theology. In those schools of law that lack a department of philosophical jurisprudence, law can easily rot away into the stale exegesis of statutes. And if philosophical theology is weak or absent, theology rots away into a barren Biblical theology composed entirely of a sterile exegesis of texts. In other words, I shall not attempt to exegete the Declaration on Religious Freedom; rather, I shall attempt to comment upon it in philosophical fashion.

The Declaration on Religious Freedom of Vatican Council II is conventionally and not altogether inaccurately interpreted as a part of the *aggiornamento*, an opening of the window that the Church may be filled with liberal air, a tardy catching up by the conscience of the Church with the more progressive and developed conscience of the world. The Church is a slow-moving conservative institution. She always takes time to adjust to new developments in a world that moves more swiftly and boldly, but after some hesitation she tends to pull herself together and catch up at last.

Many of us will feel that this is a rather humiliating description of what has occurred, but, of course, there is no particular reason why a Christian institution or a Christian man should object to being humiliated occasionally. If we can derive a little humility from the experience it will not do us very much harm. And it is certainly true that the conscience of the Church may at times fall behind the conscience of the world and that secular forces may persuade or compel Christian institutions to embark upon internal reformations to which they would have done better to move on their own initiative for purely moral, theological, and intellectual reasons. If all the Lord's people were prophets, no doubt the Church would be morally ahead of the world all the time, but it has not pleased God to create either the Church or the human race in quite that way. Thus we cannot possibly deny that this first-blush conventional interpretation of the decree does express a considerable amount of truth.

On the other hand, it does not express by any means the whole truth; indeed, there are presuppositions and implications to be found in the decree on closer analysis that the conventional interpretation misses altogether. For, in fact, the Church approaches the question of religious toleration and liberty in an entirely different way from that in which the world of our secular institutions has approached it since the eighteenth century. It is not too much to say that the reluctance of many churchmen to affirm religious toleration and liberty as basic principles is very largely due to an amply justified suspicion that the comparatively easy reception of such notions in the secular world is by no means altogether free from seriously misleading philosophical presuppositions.

The usual notion of toleration and religious freedom has been based on hedonism, skepticism, and, in consequence, apathy. The world began to move over to ideas of toleration after the bloody religious wars of the seventeenth century. These wars, some minds concluded explicitly, but more often unconsciously, were the result of too passionate and too convinced forms of faith. If men could only be persuaded to believe less wholeheartedly and entertain at least a grain of wholesome skepticism, they would do much less harm to each other. Nowadays, we seem to be living through a sort of political seventeenth century, with the wars of the rival ideologies, capitalism, communism, fascism, and whatnot filling the world with even more blood and horror than the wars of religion once did. Will all this lead, perhaps in the next century, to a period of political skepticism and apathy? There are certainly some signs that it may, that out of communism and capitalism alike there will emerge new types of government centering around a professional managerial class of skilled administrators, whose debt to any particular political ideology will be merely superficial. Perhaps this new ruling class will be men who understand and sympathize with each other so naturally and care so little about the official ideologies of their societies that they will be able to institute and organize without difficulty a lengthy period of world peace not unlike the first century or so after Augustus had established the Roman Empire.

More profoundly, the eighteenth-century movements in the direction of toleration were based upon a kind of dogmatic skepticism—if a resort to such a paradox as "dogmatic skepticism" may be pardoned. It is supposed by many men—indeed, it is assumed by many philosophers to be the one genuinely philosophical affirmation that is possible for men—that the human mind is such that no man can ever be certain of anything whatever. Man's relation to the actualities and the realities of the life he lives and the universe in which he lives is so ambiguous and remote that he is never truly at home with anything, and all his inadequate apprehensions are subject to grave doubt. Existentially, this leads to a picture of man as a kind of alien intruder in the cosmos (we do not know whence) whose intellectual and emotional alienation from absolutely everything is not an unhappy accident, but the inevitable result of the workings of his nature. Such a being is precariously related to life and dare never confide in the apparent truth of even the most vivid impression or most comprehensively lucid and intelligent affirmation.

From such a point of view, total skepticism is the only adequate and logical human philosophy. It points toward the conclusion, very familiar to the gracefully bored intellectualism of the eighteenth century, which is by no means dead yet, that the true hallmark of authentic civilization and a genuinely civilized man is polite and tolerant apathy. Many a passage in a philosopher such as David Hume illustrates the authority and extent of this kind of eighteenth century prejudice.

In a world that has assumed for so long that the only possible basis for toleration is a combination of hedonism and skepticism, theological thinkers may perhaps be pardoned for assuming that, even though toleration must be practiced, it cannot be affirmed in principle by those who believe in the possibility of truth and certainty, and the virtues of intellectual passion. Psychological certainty occurs frequently in human existence, but belief in that certainty so often proves unwarranted that it is easy to speculate that it may perhaps never be warranted. In the past many rationalist philosophers and theologians—I use the term "rationalist" to indicate a recognized philosophical party, and not to include all forms of intelligent opinion whatsoever—have believed that at least a proportion of these human psychological certainties can be logically demonstrated and transformed by such a demonstration into philosophical certainties. This is doubted by many people, but we should not suppose that if we reject this rationalistic thesis we have thereby necessarily disposed of the problem of certainty.

In ordinary life certainty is produced not so much by the solitary incidence of some one positive and indicative factor, but rather by the coincidence of a plurality of such factors. For example, if I seem to see some object before my eyes my certainty that it is really there is greatly increased and confirmed if I am able to stretch out my hand and touch it as well as see it. I may take this as one "haptic" experience in which there is a coordination and integration of visual and tactile data, but, in fact, it is two separate experiences, each of which supports and confirms the other. At the other end of the scale, what produces philosophical conviction is not the power of a single demonstrative argument, but the assembling together of a wide variety of arguments that are drawn from different strands of human experience, but that all point toward the same conclusion of a particular hypothesis. If at the same time we are able to supply systematic and withering refutations of every possible alternative to the indicated hypothesis, the result of such a coincidence of philosophical considerations may very well be something so closely akin to certainty that it becomes practically impossible to distinguish it from certainty.

Again, for many men, especially for relatively intelligent people who lack philosophical training, inclination, and skill, what conduces to the notion of certainty is the repeated experience of the consequences of forgetting, ignoring, and neglecting a certain specific form of truth. Apparently there are modes of truth, types of validity, categories of duty and obligation, that we depart from only at the cost of forfeiting both communal and personal integrity. This is a consideration that arises again and again out of the prophetic interpretation of human history. Although men constantly revolt against a prophetic interpretation of their history, it is also true that the ordinary interpretation of history tends to confirm slowly but in the long run a prophetic interpretation of history.

Thus by many pathways do we converge upon certainty. Men come to certainty when they are most authentically healthy themselves and retreat from it when they are imprisoned and enslaved by highly abstract and dry-as-dust systems of philosophical criticism that persuade them that however certain they may feel about something it is not philosophically acceptable to describe the experience in quite those terms of certainty. In such a mood everything becomes doubtful in theory even though many things are taken to be quite certain in practice. In practice, human beings find that they can be certain about apparently incompatible things that, nevertheless, seem to them overwhelmingly evident. Oddly enough, if I am certain about nothing I have no particular reason for being skeptical about anything. A skeptical father was once explaining to his small son the manifest intellectual duty of cultivating a universal skepticism, "Never be sure of anything, my boy," he said. "Only the fool ever says that he is certain." "Are you quite sure that's true?" asked the boy. "Yes, my son," replied the father. "I am quite certain of it."

But if certainty is possible it does not necessarily follow that intolerance and bloodshed are inevitable. It all depends upon what it is that we are certain about. I once visited an English university as the principal speaker at what was described as an anticommunist week-end. I suppose it was a kind of right-wing teach-in. At this particular university the Communist society was unusually strong, and I must say that the Communists attended the lectures in large numbers and greatly contributed to a very successful week-end. I remember especially the young

secretary of the Communist society in the university. She
was a very pretty girl, rather expensively dressed, with a
shapely pink face framed by long curls. She was rather
like the colored picture on a box of chocolates, and I
imagine that many a stout male heart melted at the very
sight of her.

In one of the discussions some reference was made to
such events as the destruction of the kulaks under Stalin,
and the driving of the peasants against their will into the
collective farms. During those troubled years it would
appear that several thousand Ukrainians met their death.
The secretary was asked how she would defend communism against the charge of causing so much blood and
woe. Several of the Communists present declared that
these things never occurred. But our pretty young lady
was made of sterner stuff. She quite agreed that these
regrettable events had taken place, but, she said, "If we
are absolutely certain that communism is going to make
all mankind infinitely happy forever why should we be
bothered by a few million violent deaths here and now?"
Such a sentiment delivered in a sweet voice by such a
glamorous young lady came, I must confess, as a bit of
a shock.

Suppose, on the other hand, that the object of certain
apprehension is the God of justice and love, who proposes
to create fredom, freedom even to ignore justice and to
repel love, and who sets us the example of steadfastly
respecting freedom Himself wherever He has made it.
Then surely we may say that what we are certain about
is precisely God who imposes upon us the necessity of
patience and toleration, so that our respect for the liberty
of every human creature is indeed a great grace from

Him. Thus we are able to move from a toleration that is based on skepticism to a toleration that is imposed and necessitated by faith. No intolerant faith can be a faith in the living God who creates freedom, wills freedom, Himself respects freedom, and to all His servants commands respect for freedom. Intolerant, persecuting faith is not Christian faith. To say this is no doubt to repudiate much of our history, but, inevitably, in a fallen world every man must repudiate much of his history. It is when toleration is compatible with wholehearted conviction that it ceases to be the ally of ignoble apathy and the enemy of authentic intellectual passion.

We may note also that faith in the living God proclaims the certain and central reality of one about whom all our beliefs, though profoundly valid, are necessarily inadequate. There are two kinds of agnosticism. There is the agnosticism of apathy and alienation: man is of such a character that he is inevitably cut off from truth by his very nature. What, such an agnostic may say, has a poor little creature like man to do with truth? Let him content himself with relatively expedient formulas and leave truth for the gods, if gods there be. On the other hand there is also an agnosticism that compels a man to be a nonbeliever not in the sense of hesitating to affirm truth but, on the contrary, in a sense of frankly recognizing that the truth he has affirmed passes beyond his powers of understanding. He who affirms God knows well that he must be somewhat agnostic about his conviction. It is becoming once more a commonplace of philosophical theology that no image of God can be interpreted literally, that all concepts of God, though they may point in the right direction, are necessarily inadequate, and that God is indeed beyond all possibility of definition. Books like Robinson's *Honest to God* do little more in their best moments, which it must be confessed are rather few and far between, than reinforce what Aquinas and the great representatives of that tradition have already expressed so well. We are not so skeptical as not to be certain of anything. But our central certainty is of so momentous and boundless a character as to make us somewhat skeptical of our capacity to be much more than certain about it.

Thus, he who proclaims God has affirmed the absolute existence of a reality that must humble us into at least a relative agnosticism concerning the characteristic depths and splendors inevitable in so vast and momentous a being. Even St. Paul is in this sense an agnostic when he cries, "O depth of wealth, wisdom and knowledge in God! How unsearchable his judgments, how untraceable his ways . . . Source, Guide, and Goal of all that is—to Him be glory forever!" (Romans 11:33,36).

But there is another reason why it is absolutely necessary for the Church to affirm religious liberty of a quite different character. In a world that lacks religious liberty, the integrity of the act of faith always lies under a heavy cloud of suspicion. Thus we notice in not a few contemporary histories of Western philosophy that the Christian faith of many of the great philosophers, e.g., Descartes, is explained away by non-Christian and even anti-Christian commentators in terms of their desire to avoid trouble with persecuting religious authorities. Descartes was a man who aroused in Fr. Mersenne and other Jesuits the hope that he was to be the new Aquinas of the new age. God is absolutely central to his entire philosophical system.

Fr. Mersenne and his companions would hardly have been so confident about him had they supposed that he was anything but wholehearted in his adhesion to the Catholic faith, and they, after all, knew Descartes intimately. There is, in fact, not the slightest reason to doubt the sincerity of his Christian conviction. Nevertheless, the very fact that his was the century during which Galileo met with so many misfortunes—Descartes and Galileo were contemporaries—enables philosophers like Bertrand Russell to entertain a very plausible skepticism about the integrity of the Cartesian faith. It is vitally important to the Church not only that faith be sincere but that it be seen and known by all to be sincere. This is impossible in any social system in which religious liberty is violated.

Religious liberty is thus vital to the integrity of the act of faith, and the integrity of the act of faith is vital to the authenticity of the spiritual life of the Church. It was high time that a Christian authority of supreme importance recognize and emphatically declare that only in an atmosphere of inviolable religious liberty can the Church hope to teach and commend her faith with innate spiritual authority, and that only in an atmosphere of cordiality and respect can men listen to and weigh the Declaration on Religious Freedom with reverent candor and without fear.

The Grounds for

Religious Freedom

GEORGE VAN MASSENHOVE, S.J.

MINE is the honor to conclude this discussion. An honor indeed. As in fireworks, the end is supposed to be the "bouquet." *Finis coronat opus*, the end crowns the work. But it is an honor not without dangers. How will it be possible not to disillusion, how possible, after so many brilliant comments, to present anything new on a subject that has been explored to the last corner?

In following my predecessors, I am aware that this essay will be a summary of the themes treated by them. So I present it to the reader as a kind of conclusion, as a compendium, of what the average-thinking Catholic, combining faith with common sense and an awareness of the facts of life, can carry home with him. But I must warn the reader that I speak from a European background, as one who attended the Vatican Council and heard the views expressed there by people coming from all over the world. Therefore, some of my comments may not seem relevant to the American situation, but as Catholics we have to take the whole world into account.

My topic, "The Grounds for Religious Freedom," I understand to mean not only the already discussed considerations about human dignity *in se* but the basic requirements of the Christian revelation *in se*. Those are, as you know, the fundamental reasons given in the Council declaration, and it is impossible to abstract from them. Rather than "reasons," the word "grounds" is used. That means, I think, reasons drawn from concrete situations, not from abstract considerations. Moreover, abstractions have done much harm in this matter.[1]

So, let me start from some fundamental facts of today's social life. In that context I confess my Catholic faith. From a synthesis of both I will define what religious liberty has to be *in concreto*, and why. First, let us consider some fundamental features of today's society. It is pluralistic: men and human groups with different views on life live next to and mixed in with each other. This is mainly due to internationalization. States get connected through a dense net of treaties; cultures influence one another; whatever happens somewhere finds an echo everywhere; ideas spread and find adherents everywhere. Society is becoming secularized. Secularization can be defined as "engagement in the immediateness of ordinary life," [2] that is, a preponderant, if not exclusive, concern about solving the problems of earthly life as such. And society is personalist, at least in theory. It avows fundamental "liberty and equality of human persons, without any distinction based on race, color, sex, language, creed, political or other conviction." [3] There is a growing consciousness also more in theory than in fact, that people are to be treated as adult personalities. Thus far the analysis of today's society.

In this context of life I confess my Catholic faith. I acknowledge the fact that God calls every man to adhere freely to Him by letting himself be integrated into Christ, God's son made man, and that God entrusted the Catholic Church with the fullness of means that assures the communication of God to those who live until the Lord comes. I confess that this call of God gives meaning to human existence.

The question then is: in view of these facts, the historical context and the order of salvation, what is to be the juridical status of religion in society. Or what should be the attitude of public authorities toward religious matters? Let us first exclude some conceptions that originate from an "abstract principle" and contradict one or another of the mentioned facts. A first conception posits that the state has to protect true religion while curbing, even fighting, all others. The alleged reason for this point of view is that the obligation of the state is *ex justitia*, since only truth has right and error does not. It is useless wasting time refuting this frequently expounded sophism. But, it is insisted, that at least public worship and the propaganda of false religions must be forbidden [4] because the state must foster the common good. Yet the well-understood pursuit of happiness embraces the development of all values that are present in society, including, of course, respect for truth and pursuit of man's ultimate destiny. What offends those values has to be fought by the state. Therefore . . .

One can first remark that it is utopian to want to curb every evil, even public ones, unless it be by making society into a concentration camp.[5] On the other hand, even in religious matters, some evils can be committed that ought to be prevented. So the extremely delicate question of "limits to religious freedom" is raised. We will deal with it later on.

What are we now to think about this thesis as I have formulated it? Experience provides us with the first answer: as time goes on this tends to become a false problem. In our more and more secularized society, there is a shift of interest to matters other than the dogmatic purity of religion. Modern governments have something else to do than to act as *defensor fidei*. A second answer can be made in terms of law: it exceeds the competence of the state. As Father Courtney Murray, the architect of the Council declaration, points out, one has to distinguish between society, whose aim is the common good, and the state, whose task is to secure, as a condition of the common good, the preservation of public order.[6]

But now another important point. Part of the public order is public peace, which normally depends on religious homogeneity. Blessed is the nation that knows only one religion. One people, one religion—this is the ideal. Let us first remark that this is a typically pre-Christian conception. The Jews thought like this; see the Old Testament texts. The Greeks thought like this; Socrates was sentenced to death because he did not worship the gods of the city.[7] The Roman emperors who persecuted the Christians thought like this. Even now, outside Christianity, this is the common conception. It is a confusion between religion and nationality.

As a Christian I have to reject it. Christ founded his Church on a quite different basis. He asked from every single person a free adherence. It is true that he formed these followers into a community with its own leaders, the people of God, but this people embraced those who "are not born of any human stock, or by the fleshly desire of a human father, but the offspring of God himself." [8]

Indeed, many centuries passed—as the Council declaration acknowledges—before the old tribal view and the resulting instinctive intolerance gave way to the evangelical conception.[9] I mean the view that sees state and church as two *societates perfectae*, that is, two orders of reality with quite divergent competencies. The state as an institution orders human activities with a view to the "categorical future," to use Karl Rahner's terms, the future within the data of human experience. The church gives the deeper motivation of human deeds with an eye to the "absolute future." [10]

Moreover, one can seriously doubt if religious homogeneity is in fact an ideal. For national solidity, it is simply not required. I do not need to prove this to Americans. Many nations that show the greatest cohesion and stability are pluralistic.[11] As for the Catholic Church, identification with nationality and establishment as a state religion that enjoys special privileges proves rather a curse than a blessing. It fosters immobility, laziness, and careerism on the part of the clergy, and superficiality, formalism, and hypocrisy on the part of the flock. Ask the chaplains of Spanish immigrant workers and you will hear terrifying statistics on their religious practice abroad. Among the fervent German-speaking Catholics, there is one exception, those jeeringly called "Boemisch Katholisch," the former inhabitants of Sudetenland from the former Hapsburg empire where the Church was for centuries established.

Let me add here that the *cuius regio, illius et religio*

principle, somewhat understandable when even small states were closed entities, is now absolutely outdated in this age of internationalism, ecumenism, and world-wide mission.

A second conception, widespread in this age of secularization, declares that the state may not interfere with religion. This position is defended from various premises. The most general one is that religion does not deserve any consideration. As Sartre expresses it: "God is a useless problem." For the common good it would be better if religion could be liquidated. Here too, the distinction between state and society is neglected. On the pretext that the state has nothing to do with religion, the proponents of this principle try to ban it from public life by the interdiction of religious dress, institutions, publications, associations, and even worship. Under the cloak of theoretical declarations of religious freedom there is in fact sheer persecution. That is what happened in the nineteenth century under allegedly "liberal" governments in Europe and Latin America.[12] It is even worse now in Communist-dominated countries. As a Christian I have to protest against those attacks on man's true happiness and destiny.

In a lesser form, some governments, though not against religion, think they have to abstract from it. They see it as their duty to foster certain aspects of social morality, such as the sense of solidarity, justice, discipline, courtesy, and so on, but toward religion they keep neutral.

It is unrealistic not to acknowledge in fact, through legislative measures, the moral and cultural influence of the great religions, provided, of course, that they prove that they really deserve esteem and that they contribute to the social and earthly life. Here we see, by the way, the importance of implementing vigorously the Pastoral Constitution on the Church in the Modern World.[13]

Some Catholic purists advocate a completely secular state, in order to keep the Church poor and pure. No earthly advantage should make Church leaders "bourgeois." They go even further and say that all Christians must remain loyal to Christ and his Church merely by inner and purely religious motivation, without the least moral pressure from public life, which would be the case if the state should seem to encourage religion. This appears to us a concession to an almost naive pseudo-personalism—as if all humans were really mature and adult personalities, as if weak good will did not need some encouragement from favorable circumstances.[14]

In the light of what has been said, I will try to formulate some practical conclusions. As a Catholic I hope that the whole of human society will some day be identical with the people of God, the Church. But I am afraid that it will only happen on the Day of Judgment, when there will no longer be any question of a Roman Catholic Church, but when God will have become all things to all men. To act as if on some portion of earth this day has already come is to keep up precisely the fiction of a Catholic state, of a state that, as a near contradiction in terms, has to resort to coercion in order to ensure something that has no sense if it is not the fruit of a free adherence. So I rejoice at the internationalization of society that makes the intolerant confessional state more and more impossible. I rejoice at the principle of distinction, even separation of church and state, and even at the secularization of society, by which the Church can really be the pilgrim people of God.

If, on the other hand, the state is to fulfill its real mission to ensure the conditions necessary for the common good, it must acknowledge religious bodies as social facts and protect them for their moral influence. This means that it must guarantee juridically their organizations and their properties, and allow external worship and loyal propaganda. It is also desirable that the public authorities uphold the prestige of religion through external tokens of esteem, and help the religious bodies by subsidies, be it directly or indirectly, as through tax exemptions. One necessary condition is that it be done without any discrimination on a doctrinaire basis and according to strict distributive justice. Further, the state should not interfere with the internal life of individuals and religious groups.

Experience has shown that even the most liberal declarations must contain some limitations to religious freedom. Yet the criteria are either so vague, as in the Council declaration,[15] or formulated in such a way, as in the United Nations declaration on human rights,[16] that "they are capable of putting in jeopardy those very rights." In fact, will not the interpretation that those who are in power give to it depend on their conception of morals, public order, the general good, and democracy? We prefer to say that the restrictions are attributable to the demands of the common good, that is, to the requirements of coexistence, collaboration, and coparticipation. Indeed, these notions manifest more certainly a personalist sense. They place in a prominent position the fact that, in the last instance, every limitation on the exercise of personal rights can be imposed only for the purpose of benefiting the good of the persons and of being useful for their dignity. It is a question, in fact, of the demands of coexistence of human persons as such, of the collaboration directed to the realization of values that are cultural, human, and

fruitful due to the diversity of the capacity of human persons, and of the coparticipation in the benefits of collaboration in view of the subjective culture of each and
every person.[17]

I cannot unfold now these notions, and therefore I
refer the reader to the work of my compatriot, Louis
Janssens, a specialist on the problem of person and society,
who deduces the limitations to religious freedom from the
basic requirements of the common good.

Let me only insist on the demands of coexistence. It is
up to the state to curb odious manifestations of bigotry
and aggressive intolerance, and to ensure a minimum of
public peace. But a community is badly off if it sticks to
this minimum. *Quid leges sine moribus?* What are laws
worth if behavior is not in accord with them? Legal prescriptions should be the expression of a spirit, but this does
not follow automatically. "Even the best regime can—
and this happens frequently—lead to fossilization. Instead
of fostering encounter and dialogue, the recognition of
another's freedom becomes the road to 'apartheid,' to the
formation of isolated sociological groups that live *along-
side* each other. A 'living together' that is worthy of man,
however, is not a 'living-alongside-one-another,' but is a
fruitful exchange of receiving and giving, of listening and
speaking." [18] Yet, where this open-mindedness is missing,
even peace is endangered. As long as different religious
groups eye each other suspiciously and keep their dis-
tances, and as long as a single member of a family who
changes his religion is automatically ostracized, prejudices
will reign. For example, an article on religious liberty
recently published in an Italian theological review said
in part: "And if we deplore such a religious indifference,
such a laxity and moral decadence, such a diminution of

the sense of responsibility and of the sense of sin, is it not perhaps to a large extent because of the contact and the living together, due to war and immigration, of Catholics with non-Catholics? How can he who is not well instructed in religion and solidly educated to virtue, resist and not collapse in countries where the same Creed is not recited, where people do not obey the only supreme Head (of the Church), where the sacraments are reduced to one or two, where a part of the Liturgy is abolished, and where there is a pullulation of sects and cults that are quite indulgent toward lust?" [19] As long as such a mentality prevails, the temptation will exist to encroach on another man's religious rights and to threaten his freedom.

As a Catholic I conclude: where we are a minority, we have the right to claim freedom and recognition, because of our eminent contribution to culture, morality, and the sense of the ultimate, spiritual value of mankind. Where we are the majority, we are strictly bound to grant to others the largest amount of freedom to be themselves before God. We are thought to love others, and to love somebody is, in the first place, to respect and to some extent strengthen his being different. [20]

Surely, we want all our brethren to become children of God in the Catholic Church. We speak to them the words of the apostle? "I wish that all those who are listening to me today might become what I am." [21] But we remember what our Lord revealed to John: "Here I stand knocking at the door; if anyone hears my voice and opens the door, I will come in and sit down to supper with him and he with me." [22] If our Lord and Master waits patiently until they open the door for him, we should not smash the door open and force our way in!

NOTES

1. Msgr. Jacques Leclercq notes in his excellent book on the topic: "Nous avons vu le mal qu'a fait l'abstraction. On a constamment traité de situations humaines sans se rendre compte que tout ce qui est humain se présente dans un environnement dont il faut tenir compte." J. Leclercq, *La Liberté d'Opinion et les Catholiques*, Paris, 1963, p. 353.
2. The Problem of Secularization I, DO-C papers, n. 208, p. 3.
3. *The United Nations Declaration on Human Rights*, 1948, II, 1.
4. "The argument (of St. Thomas Aquinas about equivalence of forgery and heretical propaganda) raises difficulties on the score of Church-State relationships. The secular judge is competent to judge matters concerning the currency of the realm; but whence comes his jurisdiction to judge cases involving religious doctrine? If it derives from the State, then the State would seem to be enjoying competence in the purely doctrinal field; if it derives from the Church, then civil authority would appear to be originating from the Church." Eric D'Arcy, *Conscience and Its Right to Freedom*, London and New York, 1961, p. 168.
5. "Mais c'est là une idée insoutenable. Car, tout comme l'autorité méconnaitrait les exigeances mêmes du 'bien commun' et du service qu'elle lui doit si elle prétendait assigner impérativement à chacun tout ce qu'il doit faire de positif et de bon en faveur de cette grande cause collective (ce qui reviendrait à réduire a un pur esclavage ceux même dont on se flatterait d'assurer au mieux le bonheur), ainsi ne saurait-elle sans folie vouloir prohiber et exclure par ses lois et sa police toutes les actions par lesquelles la cause du bien commun peut être plus ou moins desservie. Un pareil rêve serait même doublement insensé; et parce que la faiblesse morale des hommes rend ce projet chimérique qu'une autorité se discréditerait du seul fait qu'elle prétendrait y viser; et parce que tout effort sérieux en ce sens supposerait l'institution

d'un tel appareil d'inquisition que, loin de favoriser le bonheur général, cette entreprise deviendrait vite intolérable à tout le monde." Guy de Broglie, S.J., *Le Droit Naturel a la Liberté Religieuse*, Paris, 1964, p. 32.

6. John Courtney Murray, S.J., "The Problem of Religious Freedom," *Theological Studies*, v. 25, n. 4 (December 1964), p. 520.

7. «Σωκράτη φησὶν ἀδικεῖν ... θεοὺς οὓς ἡ πόλις νομίζει οὐ νομίζοντα ἕτερα δὲ δαιμόνια καινά ...»
Plato, *Apology of Socrates*, 23 B

8. Jo, 1, 14. ". . . Jésus s'adresse à la personne et uniquement à elle; le Nouveau Testament, et l'Evangile en particulier, ne tient aucun compte de la communauté politique.

Jésus s'adresse aux hommes en tant qu'individus. Le problème de l'adhésion à son message est un problème strictement personnel, s'adressant à chacun pour soi-même. Et Jésus s'oppose catégoriquement aux royaumes de la terre. 'Mon royaume n'est pas de la terre.' Il s'agit du royaume de Dieu, et celui-ci se présente dans des conditions toutes différentes des oeuvres humaines.

Cependant Jésus fonde une communauté humaine, une Eglise. Il groupe ses disciples sous des chefs qu'il désigne. Mais cette communauté n'a rien à voir avec l'Etat: il ne cherche pas à s'en servir et il ne cherche pas à la modifier. Il se trouve en Palestine, et il reconnaît les institutions existentes; mais celles-ci sont en dehors du plan de ses préoccupations." J. Leclercq, *op. cit.*, pp. 80-81.

9. "In the life of the People of God as it has made its pilgrim way through the vicissitudes of human history, there has at times appeared a way of acting that was hardly in accord with the spirt of the Gospel or even opposed to it." *Declaration on Religious Freedom*, NCWC edition, n. 12, pp. 11-12.

10. For the notions "absolute and categorical future" see Karl Rahner, S.J., "Christliche Zukunft des Menschen," *Orientierung* (Zürich), 29, n. 9 (May 15, 1965), p. 107.

11. "Da die Religion nicht Ziel und Zweck des Staates bildet, findet dieser auch nicht die Grundbedingung zu seiner Einheit in der Religion . . . die religiöse Einheit macht nicht die Einheit des Staates aus. Diejenigen unserer heutigen Staaten, welche diese Einheit nicht besitzen, sind darum

durchaus nicht schlechter daran; das ist unsere Stellung gegenüber der als unerlässliche Bedingung für die Einheit des Staates aufgestellten Intoleranz." Arthur Vermeersch, aus dessen bekannten Buch über die Toleranz (1912) diese Worte stammen, erinnert daran, dass eine Begründung der staatlichen Einheit in der Einheit der Religion auf der heidnischen Idee einer vollständigen Verschmelzung des politischen und religiösen Lebens beruht, die durch das Christentum und die von ihm gebrachte Scheidung der Kirche und des Staates überwunden worden ist. Die Annahme, dass die religiöse Einheit notwendig für die politische sei, würde den Staat dazu führen, "über die Religion zu bestimmen, und das ist gegen die Würde der Religion, die dem Staate wesentlich überlegen ist." Albert Hartmann, S.J., *Toleranz und Christlicher Glauben*, Frankfurt a. M., 1955, pp. 243-244.

12. "Il faut ajouter que le libéralisme se présentait incarné dans des gouvernements dits libéraux qui, de l'aveu même des libéraux d'aujourd'hui, étaient en réalité souvent fort peu libéraux: il s'agissait plutôt, en bien des cas, de radicaux, oppresseurs de la liberté de l'Eglise, auxquels on aurait pu reprocher plus d'une fois ce qu'un journal français, peu suspect de cléricalisme cependant, reprochait au government 'libéral' qui avait pris le pouvoir en Espagne en 1869: 'Il a accordé la liberté à tous les cultes sauf au seul que connaissent les Espagnols.' " R. Aubert, *La Magistère Ecclésiastique et le Libéralisme*, in *Tolérance et Communauté Humaine*, Tournai-Paris, 1952, p. 101.

13. "Concrètement, d'ailleurs, notre indépendance, comme aussi l'efficacité de notre apport catholique, dépendra beaucoup de la force de nos convictions et de notre valeur, non seulement religieuse, mais humaine et même technique. . . . Une fois de plus, la double loyauté à Dieu et aux hommes, à l'Eglise et au monde, est la loi paradoxale de notre témoignage et de l'efficacité de celui-ci." Y. Congar, O.P., *Les Conditions Théologiques d'un Pluralisme*, in *Tolérance et Communauté Humaine, op. cit.*, p. 219.

14. In his book, *L'Oraison Problème Politique* (Paris, 1965), Jean Daniélou, S.J., opposes, in a somewhat exaggerated way, these extremely idealistic views. The Church, he asserts, has to take into account those who are weak, the "poor ones,"

and tend, in order to help them, to the restoration of some kind of "Christianity," a type of society with specifically Christian features.

15. "Juridical norms which are in conformity with the objective moral order. Those norms arise out of the need for the effective safeguard of the rights of all citizens . . . for an adequate care of genuine public peace, . . . for a proper guardianship of public morality." *Op. cit.*, n. 7, p. 8.

16. "In the exercise of his rights and freedoms, everyone shall be subject only to such limitations as are determined by law solely for the purpose of securing due recognition and respect for the rights and freedoms of others and of meeting the just requirements of morality, public order and the general welfare in a democratic society." *Universal Declaration on Human Rights*, art. 29, sect. 2.

17. Louis Janssens, *Freedom of Conscience and Religious Freedom*, Staten Island, N.Y., 1966, p. 135.

18. Albert Dondeyne, *Faith and the World*, Pittsburgh, Pa., 1963, p. 288.

19. "E se deploriamo tanto indifferentismo religioso, tanta rilassatezza e decadenza morale, tanta diminuzione del senso della responsabilità della vita e del senso del peccato, non ne è forse in gran parte causa il contatto e la convivenza, anche a causa delle guerre et delle emigrazioni, dei cattolici coi non cattolici?

Chi non è bene istruito nella religione e saldamente formato alla virtù, come può resistere e non crollare in Paesi dove non si recita lo stesso Credo, non si ubbedisce a un unico Capo supremo, dove sono ridotti à uno o due i Sacramenti, ed è in parte abolita la Liturgia, e dove pullulano sette e culti assai indulgenti alle passioni?" P. Francesco M. Marchesi, "La Libertà Religiosa," *Divus Thomas*, April-June 1965, p. 197.

20. "By love and care the burden which the other is for me becomes in a sense even heavier, for love strives to establish the other in his 'otherness.'" Albert Dondeyne, *op. cit.*, p. 282.

21. Acts, 26, 29.

22. Apocalypse of John, 3, 20.

APPENDIX

Declaration on Religious Freedom: On the Right of the Person and of Communities to Social and Civil Freedom in Matters Religious

PAUL, BISHOP
SERVANT OF THE SERVANTS OF GOD
TOGETHER WITH THE FATHERS OF
THE SACRED COUNCIL
FOR EVERLASTING MEMORY

1. A sense of the dignity of the human person has been impressing itself more and more deeply on the consciousness of contemporary man.[1] And the demand is increasingly made that men should act on their own judgment, enjoying and making use of a responsible freedom, not driven by coercion but motivated by a sense of duty. The demand is also made that constitutional limits should be set to the powers of government, in order that there may be no encroachment on the rightful freedom of the person and of associations.

This demand for freedom in human society chiefly regards

---

1. Cf. *John XXIII, encyclical "Pacem in Terris," Apr. 11, 1963: AAS 55 (1963), p. 279; ibid., p. 265; Pius XII, radio message, Dec. 24, 1944: AAS 37 (1945), p. 14.*

the quest for the values proper to the human spirit. It regards, in the first place, the free exercise of religion in society.[2]

This Vatican Synod takes careful note of these desires in the minds of men. It proposes to declare them to be greatly in accord with truth and justice. To this end, it searches into the sacred tradition and doctrine of the Church—the treasury out of which the Church continually brings forth new things that are in harmony with the things that are old.

First,[3] this sacred Synod professes its belief that God himself has made known to mankind the way in which men are to

2. Vatican II has been characterized by a sense of history, an awareness of the concrete world of fact, and a disposition to see in historical facts certain "signs of the times." Hence the Declaration begins by noting two facts. The first is the recent rise of man's personal consciousness, his sense of selfhood. This increasing awareness of the dignity of the human person marks a progress of civilization. It is the good which has come out of the great evil of totalitarianism, which brutally refuses to acknowledge the reality of man's selfhood. The second fact is the related rise of man's political consciousness, his aspiration to live as a free man under a limited government which puts no obstacles to his pursuit of truth and virtue, and, in particular, leaves him unhindered in the free exercise of religion in society. (Happily, the Declaration adopts the classical phrase which the Founding Fathers likewise adopted when framing the First Amendment in 1791.)

    In thus acknowledging certain realities of contemporary life, the Declaration also establishes direct continuity with two basic doctrinal themes of John XXIII in the encyclical "Pacem in Terris": the dignity of the human person and the consequent necessity of constitutional limits to the powers of government. The language of these opening sentences, is, in fact, taken from this great encyclical.

3. The issue of religious freedom arises in the political and social order —in the order of the relationship between the people and government and between man and man. This is the order of human rights, and in it the principle of freedom is paramount. However, man's life is also lived in another order of reality—in the spiritual order of man's relationship to what is objectively true and morally good. This is the order of duty and obligation. In it a man acts freely indeed, but under moral imperatives, which bind in conscience. No man may plead "rights" in the face of the truth or claim "freedom" from the moral law. The distinction between these two orders of reality would be admitted by all men of good sense. The underlying intention of these two paragraphs of the

serve Him, and thus be saved in Christ and come to blessedness.
We believe that this one true religion subsists in the catholic
and apostolic Church, to which the Lord Jesus committed the
duty of spreading it abroad among all men. Thus He spoke to
the apostles: "Go, therefore, and make disciples of all nations,
baptizing them in the name of the Father, and of the Son, and
of the Holy Spirit, teaching them to observe all that I have
commanded you" (Mt. 28:19-20). On their part, all men are
bound to seek the truth, especially in what concerns God and
His Church, and to embrace the truth they come to know,
and to hold fast to it.

Declaration is to make this distinction clear, lest religious freedom
be made a pretext for moral anarchy.

However, the distinction is stated in Catholic terms. For the
Catholic, the "truth" is not a vague abstraction; it subsists in the
Church, is taught by the Church, is believed by the Church.
Moreover, this truth about God and about His will for men is not
the private possession of a party or sect; it is to be taught to all
men, and all nations are to be its disciples. It is not to be thrust
by force upon any man; in the order of man's relationship to
truth, coercion has no place whatsoever. Consequently, as the
Declaration will later make clear, religious freedom is an exigence
of religious truth as conceived by the Church.

On the other hand, no man may say of the religious truth which
subsists in the Church: "It is no concern of mine." Once given by
Christ to His true Church, the true religion remains the one way
in which all men are bound to serve God and save themselves.
Consequently, religious freedom is not a title to exemption from
the obligation to "observe all things whatsoever I have enjoined
upon you." In fine, a harmony exists between man's duty of free
obedience to the truth and his right to the free exercise of religion
in society. The duty does not diminish the right, nor does the
right diminish the duty.

This frank profession of Catholic faith, at the outset of the
Declaration on Religious Freedom, is in no sense at variance with
the ecumenical spirit, any more than it is at variance with the full
loyalty to the principle of religious freedom. Neither the spirit of
ecumenism nor the principle of religious freedom requires that the
Church refrain from stating publicly what she believes herself to
be. The demands of truth are no more opposed to the demands of
freedom than they are opposed to the demands of love.

This sacred Synod likewise professes its belief that it is upon the human conscience that these obligations fall and exert their binding force. The truth cannot impose itself except by virtue of its own truth, as it makes its entrance into the mind at once quietly and with power. Religious freedom, in turn, which men demand as necessary to fulfill their duty to worship God, has to do with immunity from coercion in civil society. Therefore, it leaves untouched traditional Catholic doctrine on the moral duty of men and societies toward the true religion and toward the one Church of Christ.

Over and above all this, in taking up the matter of religious freedom this sacred Synod intends to develop the doctrine of recent Popes on the inviolable rights of the human person and on the constitutional order of society.[4]

4. In no other conciliar document is it so explicitly stated that the intention of the Council is to "develop" Catholic doctrine. This is significant, since it is an avowal that the tradition of the Church is a tradition of progress in understanding the truth. The basic truth here is the concept of the "citizen" as stated by Pius XII—the man who "feels within himself a consciousness of his own personality, of his duties, and of his rights, joined with a respect for the freedom of others" (Christmas Discourse, 1945). This conception, as the Declaration will say, is deeply rooted both in the Christian tradition and in the tradition of reason. In recent times, it was Leo XIII (in "Rerum Novarum") who first began to move it, as it were, to the forefront of Catholic social teaching. Pius XII continued this development, drawing out the implications of the dignity of man in terms of his duties and rights. He also brought forward the correlative truth, that the primary function of government is to acknowledge, protect, vindicate, and facilitate the exercise of the rights of man. Both of these truths were taken up by John XXIII, chiefly in "Pacem in Terris," in which they are given an almost systematic form of statement.

However, in regard to the right of man to religious freedom, even "Pacem in Terris" is unclear and even ambiguous. What precisely does religious freedom mean? Does it find place among the inalienable rights of man? These are the questions to which, for the first time, the Church gives an unmistakably clear and entirely unambiguous answer. The Council brings forth out of the treasury of truth a doctrine that is at once new and also in harmony with traditional teaching.

I. GENERAL PRINCIPLE
OF RELIGIOUS FREEDOM

2. This Vatican Synod declares that the human person has a right to religious freedom.[5] This freedom means that all men

5. The doctrinal substance of the Declaration is stated in this paragraph, which defines what religious freedom is and affirms its status as a human—and therefore civil—right. A right is a moral claim made on others that they either give me something or do something for me or refrain from doing something. Two questions always arise. First, what is the moral claim I make on others, or in other words, what is the object or content of my right? Second, on what grounds do I make this moral claim, or in other words, what is the foundation of my right?

The Declaration first defines religious freedom in terms of its object or content. The moral claim that every man makes on others—on individuals, groups, political or social powers—is that they refrain from bringing coercion to bear on him in all matters religious. This claim is twofold. First, no man is to be forced to act in a manner contrary to his personal beliefs; second, no man is to be forcibly restrained from acting in accordance with his beliefs. The affirmation of this latter immunity is the new thing, which is in harmony with the older affirmation of the former immunity.

It is to be noted that the word "conscience," found in the Latin text, is used in its generic sense, sanctioned by usage, of "beliefs," "convictions," "persuasions." Hence the unbeliever or atheist makes with equal right this claim to immunity from coercion in religious matters. It is further to be noted that, in assigning a negative content to the right to religious freedom (that is, in making it formally a "freedom from" and not a "freedom for"), the Declaration is in harmony with the sense of the First Amendment to the American Constitution. In guaranteeing the free exercise of religion, the First Amendment guarantees to the American citizen immunity from all coercion in matters religious. Neither the Declaration nor the American Constitution affirms that a man has a right to believe what is false or to do what is wrong. This would be moral nonsense. Neither error nor evil can be the object of a right, only what is true and good. It is, however, true and good that a man should enjoy freedom from coercion in matters religious.

This brings up the second question, concerning the foundation of the right. The reason why every man may claim immunity from coercion in matters religious is precisely his inalienable dig-

are to be immune from coercion on the part of indivduals or
of social groups and of any human power, in such wise that in
matters religious no one is to be forced to act in a manner
contrary to his own beliefs. Nor is anyone to be restrained
from acting in accordance with his own beliefs, whether
privately or publicly, whether alone or in association with
others, within due limits.

The Synod further declares that the right to religious freedom has its foundation in the very dignity of the human person, as this dignity is known through the revealed Word of
God and by reason itself.[6] This right of the human person to
religious freedom is to be recognized in the constitutional law
whereby society is governed. Thus it is to become a civil right.

It is in accordance with their dignity as persons—that is,
beings endowed with reason and free will and therefore privi-

---

nity as a human person. Surely, in matters religious, if anywhere,
the free human person is required and entitled to act on his own
judgment and to assume personal responsibility for his action or
omission. A man's religious decisions, or his decision against religion, are inescapably his own. No one else can make them for
him, or compel him to make this decision or that, or restrain him
from putting his decisions into practice, privately or publicly,
alone or in company with others. In all these cases, the dignity
of man would be diminished because of the denial to him of that
inalienable responsibility for his own decisions and actions which
is the essential counterpart of his freedom.

It is worth noting that the Declaration does not base the right
to the free exercise of religion on "freedom of conscience." Nowhere does this phrase occur. And the Declaration nowhere lends
its authority to the theory for which the phrase frequently stands,
namely, that I have the right to do what my conscience tells me
to do, simply because my conscience tells me to do it. This is a
perilous theory. Its particular peril is subjectivism—the notion that,
in the end, it is my conscience, and not the objective truth, which
determines what is right or wrong, true or false.

6. Cf. *John XXIII*, encyclical "*Pacem in Terris*," *Apr. 11, 1963: AAS*
55 (1963), pp. 260-261; Pius XII, radio message, Dec. 24, 1942:
AAS 35 (1943), p. 19; Pius XI, encyclical "Mit Brennender Sorge,"
Mar. 14, 1937: AAS 29 (1937), p. 160; Leo XIII, encyclical "Lib-
ertas Praestantissimum," June 20, 1888: Acts of Leo XIII 8 (1888),
pp. 237-238.

leged to bear personal responsibility—that all men should be at once impelled by nature and also bound by a moral obligation to seek the truth, especially religious truth. They are also bound to adhere to the truth, once it is known, and to order their whole lives in accord with the demands of truth.

However, men cannot discharge these obligations in a manner in keeping with their own nature unless they enjoy immunity from external coercion as well as psychological freedom. Therefore, the right to religious freedom has its foundation, not in the subjective disposition of the person, but in his very nature. In consequence, the right to this immunity continues to exist even in those who do not live up to their obligation of seeking the truth and adhering to it. Nor is the exercise of this right to be impeded, provided that the just requirements of public order are observed.[7]

3. Further light is shed on the subject if one considers that

7. It was necessary for the Council to present an argument for the principle of religious freedom, lest anyone should mistakenly think that the Church was accepting religious freedom merely on pragmatic grounds or as a concession to contemporary circumstances. However, it was not the intention of the Council to affirm that the argument, as made in the text, is final and decisive. Complete and systematic study of the arguments for religious freedom is a task left to the scholars of the Church, working in ecumenical spirit with scholars of other religious Communities, and in humanist spirit with scholars of no religious convictions who are concerned with the exigencies of human dignity. The Council merely presents certain lines or elements of argument. It will be sufficient here to indicate the structure.

First, in this paragraph, the objective foundation of the right to religious freedom is presented in terms that should be intelligible and acceptable to all men, including non-believers. The simple essence of the matter is that man, being intelligent and free, is to be a responsible agent. Inherent in his very nature, therefore, is an exigency for freedom from coercion, especially in matters religious. Therefore, in the following three paragraphs, an argument is suggested that will appeal to those who believe in God, in objective order of truth and morality, and in the obligation to seek the truth, form one's conscience, and obey its dictates. To the man who so believes, it will be evident that no one is to be forced or constrained to act against his own conscience (here conscience has its technical meaning).

the highest norm of human life is the divine law—eternal, objective, and universal—whereby God orders, directs, and governs the entire universe and all the ways of the human community, by a plan conceived in wisdom and love. Man has been made by God to participate in this law, with the result that, under the gentle disposition of divine Providence, he can come to perceive ever increasingly the unchanging truth. Hence every man has the duty, and therefore the right, to seek the truth in matters religious, in order that he may with prudence form for himself right and true judgments of conscience, with the use of all suitable means.

Truth, however, is to be sought after in a manner proper to the dignity of the human person and his social nature. The inquiry is to be free, carried on with the aid of teaching or instruction, communication, and dialogue. In the course of these, men explain to one another the truth they have discovered, or think they have discovered, in order thus to assist one another in the quest for truth. Moreover, as the truth is discovered, it is by a personal assent that men are to adhere to it.

On his part, man perceives and acknowledges the imperatives of the divine law through the mediation of conscience. In all his activity a man is bound to follow his conscience faithfully, in order that he may come to God, for whom he was created.

Two further arguments are advanced to show that a man may not be restrained from acting according to his conscience. First, by reason of man's social nature, inner acts of religion require external expression; hence their external expression enjoys the same immunity from coercion as the inner acts themselves. Second, there is the "further consideration" that no right resides in government to command or inhibit acts of religion, which by their nature lie beyond the reach of government.

American theorists are generally disposed to relate religious freedom to a general theory of constitutional government, limited by the rights of man, and to the concept of civic equality. The Declaration, however, lays less stress on this political argument than it does on the ethical foundations of the right itself. In any event, the elements of the political argument are stated in later Articles (6 and 7). And one is free to construct the argument in the form which may seem more convincing.

It follows that he is not to be forced to act in a manner contrary to his conscience. Nor, on the other hand, is he to be restrained from acting in accordance with his conscience, especially in matters religious.

For, of its very nature, the exercise of religion consists before all else in those internal, voluntary, and free acts whereby man sets the course of his life directly toward God. No merely human power can either command or prohibit acts of this kind.[8]

However, the social nature of man itself requires that he should give external expression to his internal acts of religion; that he should participate with others in matters religious; that he should profess his religion in community. Injury, therefore, is done to the human person and to the very order established by God for human life, if the free exercise of religion is denied in society when the just requirements of public order do not so require.

There is a further consideration. The religious acts whereby men, in private and in public and out of a sense of personal conviction, direct their lives to God transcend by their very nature the order of terrestrial and temporal affairs. Government, therefore, ought indeed to take account of the religious life of the people and show it favor, since the function of government is to make provision for the common welfare. However, it would clearly transgress the limits set to its power were it to presume to direct or inhibit acts that are religious.
4. The freedom or immunity from coercion in matters religious which is the endowment of persons as individuals is also to be recognized as their right when they act in community. Religious bodies are a requirement of the social nature both of man and of religion itself.[9]

8. Cf. *John XXIII, encyclical "Pacem in Terris," Apr. 11, 1963: AAS 55 (1963), p. 270; Paul VI, radio message, Dec. 22, 1964: AAS 57 (1965), pp. 181-182.*
9. The freedoms listed here are those which the Catholic Church claims for herself. The Declaration likewise claims them for all Churches and religious Communities. Lest there be misunderstanding, however, it is necessary to recall here the distinction between

Provided the just requirements of public order are observed, religious bodies rightfully claim freedom in order that they may govern themselves according to their own norms, honor the Supreme Being in public worship, assist their members in the practice of the religious life, strengthen them by instruction, and promote institutions in which they may join together for the purpose of ordering their own lives in accordance with their religious principles.

Religious bodies also have the right not to be hindered, either by legal measures or by administrative action on the part of government, in the selection, training, appointment, and transferral of their own ministers, in communicating with religious authorities and communities abroad, in erecting buildings for religious purposes, and in the acquisition and use of suitable funds or properties.

Religious bodies also have the right not to be hindered in their public teaching and witness to their faith, whether by the spoken or by the written word. However, in spreading religious faith and in introducing religious practices, everyone ought at all times to refrain from any manner of action which might seem to carry a hint of coercion or of a kind of

---

the content or object of the right and its foundation. The content or object always remains freedom from coercion in what concerns religious belief, worship, practice or observance, and public testimony. Hence the content of the right is the same both for the Catholic Church and for other religious bodies. In this sense, the Church claims nothing for herself which she does not also claim for them. The matter is different, however, with regard to the foundation of the right. The Catholic Church claims freedom from coercive interference in her ministry and life on grounds of the divine mandate laid upon her by Christ Himself (cf. below, note 13). It is Catholic faith that no other Church or Community may claim to possess this mandate in all its fullness. In this sense, the freedom of the Church is unique, proper to herself alone, by reason of its foundation. In the case of other religious Communities, the foundation of the right is the dignity of the human person, which requires that men be kept free from coercion, when they act in community, gathered into Churches, as well as when they act alone.

persuasion that would be dishonorable or unworthy, especially when dealing with poor or uneducated people. Such a manner of action would have to be considered an abuse of one's own right and a violation of the right of others.[10]

In addition, it comes within the meaning of religious freedom that religious bodies should not be prohibited from freely undertaking to show the special value of their doctrine in what concerns the organization of society and the inspiration of the whole of human activity.[11] Finally, the social nature of man and the very nature of religion afford the foundation of the right of men freely to hold meetings and to establish educational, cultural, charitable, and social organizations, under the impulse of their own religious sense.

5. Since the family [12] is a society in its own original right, it has the right freely to live its own domestic religious life under the guidance of parents. Parents, moreover, have the right to determine, in accordance with their own relogous beliefs, the kind of religious education that their children are to receive.

10. It is customary to distinguish between "Christian witness" and "proselytism" and to condemn the latter. This distinction is made in the text here. Proselytism is a corruption of Christian witness by appeal to hidden forms of coercion or by a style of propaganda unworthy of the gospel. It is not the use but the abuse of the right to religious freedom.

11. Implicitly rejected here is the outmoded notion that "religion is a purely private affair" or that "the Church belongs in the sacristy." Religion is relevant to the life and action of society. Therefore religious freedom includes the right to point out this social relevance of religious belief.

12. The internal structure of family relationships and the general style of family life vary widely throughout the world. Still greater variety is exhibited in the organization of school systems, in their relation to the family, to society, and to government, and in the religious and ideological content, or lack thereof, of their teaching. In consequence, the Declaration had to confine itself to a few principles of universal import, which would enforce its doctrinal line—freedom from coercion. To descend to further detail would be to enter the realm of policy, in which contingent circumstances play a determinant role.

Government, in consequence, must acknowledge the right of parents to make a genuinely free choice of schools and of other means of education. The use of this freedom of choice is not to be made a reason for imposing unjust burdens on parents, whether directly or indirectly. Besides, the rights of parents are violated if their children are forced to attend lessons or instruction which are not in agreement with their religious beliefs. The same is true if a single system of education, from which all religious formation is excluded, is imposed upon all.

6. The common welfare of society consists in the entirety of those conditions of social life under which men enjoy the possibility of achieving their own perfection in a certain fullness of measure and also with some relative ease. Hence this welfare consists chiefly in the protection of the rights,[13] and in the performance of the duties, of the human person. Therefore, the care of the right to religious freedom devolves upon the people as a whole, upon social groups, upon government, and upon the Church and other religious Communities, in virtue of the duty of all toward the common welfare, and in the manner proper to each.[14]

13. Cf. *John XXIII, encyclical "Mater et Magistra," May 15, 1961: AAS 53 (1961), p. 417; idem, encyclical "Pacem in Terris," Apr. 11, 1963: AAS 55 (1963), p. 273.*

14. The development of Catholic doctrine which the Declaration promised has already shown itself in the clear definition of religious freedom as a human right and in the firm claim that all Churches and religious Communities are entitled to equal freedom from coercion in what concerns religious belief, worship, practice or observance, public testimony, and the internal autonomy of the community itself. Correlative with these developments is the doctrine stated here with regard to the functions and limitations of government in what concerns religion in society. The pivotal notion is the concept of the common welfare which Leo XIII began to put forward in "Rerum Novarum," which Pius XII strongly developed, and which John XXIII defined with greater precision. The common welfare "chiefly consists in the protection of the rights, and in the performance of the duties, of the human person," who is to be the agent of the processes of society and their beneficiary. The care of the common welfare is the common

The protection and promotion of the inviolable rights of man ranks among the essential duties of government.[15] Therefore, government is to assume the safeguard of the religious freedom of all its citizens, in an effective manner, by just laws

---

task of all elements within society—individuals, groups, religious bodies, government—each in the way proper to itself.

In a special way, the care of the common good—that is to say, the care of the rights of man—devolves upon government. Consequently, in what concerns religion in society, government has a duty that is twofold. The first duty is to acknowledge the human right to religious freedom, and effectively to protect it and vindicate it against violation. The second duty derives from the general duty of government to assist the people in the performance of their duties; in this case, it is to show a general and undiscriminating favor toward religion in society (cf. above, note 3, at the end) and to assist in the creation of conditions that will help, not hinder, the people in the exercise of their religious rights and in the performance of their religious duties. This latter duty is stated with considerable generality, because the appropriate means for its performance will vary within diverse circumstances.

The concern of the Council was, first, to make entirely clear the duty of government toward religious freedom as a human right, and secondly, to make sufficiently clear the function of government with regard to religion itself as a perfection of the human person and as a social value. This latter function is not easy to define with precision. It is chiefly a matter of avoiding extremes. On the one hand, government is forbidden to assume the care of religious truth as such, or jurisdiction over religious worship or practice, or the task of judging the truth or value of religious propaganda. Otherwise it would exceed its competence, which is confined to affairs of the temporal and terrestrial order. On the other hand, government is likewise forbidden to adopt toward religion an attitude of indifference or skepticism, much less hostility. Otherwise it would betray its duty to the human person, for whom religion is the highest good, and also to the temporal and terrestrial welfare of society, whose content is not merely material but also moral and spiritual. Here then is the principle for finding the golden mean between the extremes.

15. Cf. *John XXIII, encyclical "Pacem in Terris," Apr. 11, 1963: AAS 55 (1963), pp. 273-274; Pius XII, radio message, June 1, 1941: AAS 33 (1941), p. 200.*

and by other appropriate means. Government is also to help create conditions favorable to the fostering of religious life, in order that the people may be truly enabled to exercise their religious rights and to fulfill their religious duties, and also in order that society itself may profit by the moral qualities of justice and peace which have their origin in men's faithfulness to God and to His holy will.[16]

If, in view of peculiar circumstances obtaining among certain peoples, special legal recognition is given in the constitutional order of society to one religious body, it is at the same time imperative that the right of all citizens and religious bodies to religious freedom should be recognized and made effective in practice.[17]

Finally, government is to see to it that the equality of citizens before the law, which is itself an element of the common welfare, is never violated for religious reasons [18] whether openly or covertly. Nor is there to be discrimination among citizens.

It follows that a wrong is done when government imposes upon its people, by force or fear or other means, the profession or repudiation of any religion, or when it hinders men from joining or leaving a religious body. All the more is it a violation of the will of God and of the sacred rights of the

16. Cf. Leo XIII, encyclical *"Immortale Dei,"* Nov. *1, 1885: AAS 18 (1885), p. 161.*

17. This paragraph is carefully phrased. The Council did not wish to condemn the institution of "establishment," the notion of a "religion of the state." A respectable opinion maintains that the institution is compatible with full religious freedom. On the other hand, the Council did not wish to canonize the institution. A respectable opinion holds that establishment is always a threat to religious freedom. Furthermore, the Council wished to insinuate that establishment, at least from the Catholic point of view, is a matter of historical circumstance, not of theological doctrine. For all these reasons the text deals with the issue in conditional terms.

18. This statement about equality before the law as an element of the common welfare has an accent of newness in official Catholic statements. It is important for the construction of the full argument for religious freedom.

person and the family of nations, when force is brought to
bear in any way in order to destroy or repress religion, either
in the whole of mankind or in a particular country or in a
specific community.[19]

7. The right to religious freedom is exercised in human society;
hence its exercise is subject to certain regulatory norms.[20] In

19. This condemnation of religious persecution is couched in temperate
    terms and without naming the guilty. However, the reference to
    totalitarian regimes of Communist inspiration is unmistakable.

20. It is a matter of common sense that the exercise of all freedoms in
    society must be subject to certain regulatory norms. The Declara-
    tion states first the moral norm—the principle of personal and
    social responsibility. Its restraints, of course, are self-imposed.
    More difficult is the question of the juridical norm which should
    control the action of government in limiting or inhibiting the
    exercise of the right to religious freedom. (Note that the right
    itself is always inalienable, never to be denied; only the exercise
    of the right is subject to control in particular instances.) The
    norm cannot be the common welfare, since the common welfare
    requires that human rights should be protected, not limited, in
    their exercise. Hence the Declaration adopts the concept of public
    order. The concept has good warrant in constitutional law. How-
    ever, it is more frequently used than defined. The Declaration
    undertakes to define it. In doing so, it makes a contribution to the
    science of law and jurisprudence.
        First, the requirements of public order are not subject to arbi-
    trary definiton—at the hands, say, of tyrannical governments,
    which might abuse the concept for their own ends. The public
    order of society is a part of the universal moral order; its re-
    quirements must be rooted in moral law. Second, public order
    exhibits a threefold content. First, the order of society is essen-
    tially an order of justice, in which the rights of all citizens are
    effectively safeguarded, and provision is made for peaceful settle-
    ment of conflicts of rights. Second, the order of society is a
    political order, an order of peace ("domestic tranquillity" is the
    American constitutional phrase). Public peace, however, is not the
    result of repressive action by the police. It is, in the classic con-
    cept, the work of justice; it comes about, of itself, when the
    demands of justice are met, and when orderly processes exist for
    airing and settling grievances. Third, the order of society is a
    moral order, at least in the sense that certain minimal standards of
    public morality are enforced at all.
        Public order therefore is constituted by these three values—

the use of all freedoms, the moral principle of personal and social responsibility is to be observed. In the exercise of their rights, individual men and social groups are bound by the moral law to have respect both for the rights of others and for their own duties toward others and for the common welfare of all. Men are to deal with their fellows in justice and civility.

Furthermore, society has the right to defend itself against possible abuses committed on pretext of freedom of religion. It is the special duty of government to provide this protection. However, government is not to act in arbitrary fashion or in an unfair spirit of partisanship. Its action is to be controlled by juridical norms which are in conformity with the objective moral order.

These norms arise out of the need for effective safeguard of the rights of all citizens and for peaceful settlement of conflicts of rights. They flow from the need for an adequate care of genuine public peace, which comes about when men live together in good order and in true justice. They come, finally, out of the need for a proper guardianship of public morality. These matters constitute the basic component of the common welfare: they are what is meant by public order.

For the rest,[21] the usages of society are to be the usages of

---

juridical, political, moral. They are the basic elements in the common welfare, which is a wider concept than public order. And so necessary are these three values that the coercive force of government may be enlisted to protect and vindicate them. Together they furnish a reasonable juridical criterion for coercive restriction of freedom. The free exercise of religion may not be inhibited unless proof is given that it entails some violation of the rights of others, or of the public peace, or of public morality. In these cases, in other words, a public action ceases to be a religious exercise and becomes a penal offense.

21. Secular experts may well consider this to be the most significant sentence in the Declaration. It is a statement of the basic principle of the "free society." The principle has important origins in the medieval tradition of kingship, law, and jurisprudence. But its statement by the Church has an accent of blessed newness—the

freedom in their full range. These require that the freedom of
man be respected as far as possible, and curtailed only when
and in so far as necessary.

8. Many pressures are brought to bear upon men of our day,
to the point where the danger arises lest they lose the possibility of acting on their own judgment. On the other hand, not
a few can be found who seem inclined to use the name of
freedom as the pretext for refusing to submit to authority and
for making light of the duty of obedience.

Therefore, this Vatican Synod urges everyone, especially
those who are charged with the task of educating others, to
do their utmost to form men who will respect the moral order
and be obedient to lawful authority. Let them form men too
who will be lovers of true freedom—men, in other words, who
will come to decisions on their own judgment and in the light
of truth, govern their activities with a sense of responsibility,
and strive after what is true and right, willing always to join
with others in cooperative effort.[22]

Religious freedom, therefore, ought to have this further
purpose and aim, namely, that men may come to act with

---

newness of a renewal of the tradition. The renewal, already hesi-
tantly begun by Pius XII, was strongly furthered by John XXIII.
Catholic thought had consistently held that society is to be based
upon truth (the truth of the human person), directed toward
justice, and animated by charity. In "Pacem in Terris," John
XXIII added the missing fourth term, freedom. Freedom is an end
or purpose of society, which looks to the liberation of the human
person. Freedom is the political method par excellence, whereby
the other goals of society are reached. Freedom, finally, is the
prevailing social usage, which sets the style of society. This
progress in doctrine is sanctioned and made secure by "Dignitatis
Humanae Personae."

22. The Council calls attention to the paradox of the moment. Freedom
today is threatened; freedom today is itself a threat. Hence the
Council calls for education both in the uses of freedom and in
the ways of obedience. When freedom is truly responsible, it
implies a rightful response to legitimate authority.

greater responsibility in fulfilling their duties in community
life.[23]

II. RELIGIOUS FREEDOM IN THE
LIGHT OF REVELATION

9. The declaration of this Vatican Synod on the right of man
to religious freedom has its foundation in the dignity of the
person. The requirements of this dignity have come to be
more adequately known to human reason through centuries of
experience. What is more, this doctrine of freedom has roots
in divine revelation, and for this reason Christians are bound to
respect it all the more conscientiously.

Revelation does not indeed affirm in so many words the
right of man to immunity from external coercion in matters
religious. It does, however, disclose the dignity of the human
person in its full dimensions. It gives evidence of the respect
which Christ showed toward the freedom with which man is
to fulfill his duty of belief in the Word of God. It gives us
lessons too in the spirit which disciples of such a Master ought
to make their own and to follow in every situation.

Thus, further light is cast on the general principles upon
which the doctrine of this Declaration on Religious Freedom
is based. In particular, religious freedom in society is entirely
consonant with the freedom of the act of Christian faith.[24]

23. Religious freedom is not an end in itself, but a means for the ful-
    fillment of the higher purposes of man. Its religious purpose is
    clear. But here the Council notes its social purpose. Respect for
    religious freedom rises out of a consciousness of human dignity;
    but this consciousness itself confronts man with the responsibilities
    that his freedom entails. And these responsibilities pervade the
    whole of community life.
24. The Declaration is the only conciliar document formally addressed
    to the whole world—Christian and non-Christian, religious and
    atheist. Therefore it first considers religious freedom in the light
    of reason. Moreover, in so doing it follows the structure of the
    problem itself, both theoretical and historical. Both as a principle

10. It is one of the major tenets of Catholic doctrine that man's response to God in faith must be free. Therefore no one is to be forced to embrace the Christian faith [25] against his own will.[26] This doctrine is contained in the Word of God and it was constantly proclaimed by the Fathers of the Church.[27]

---

and as a legal institution, religious freedom is less than two hundred years old. The First Amendment may claim the honor of having first clearly formulated the principle and established the institution. Only through centuries of experience, as the Declaration says, have the exigencies of the human dignity disclosed themselves to reason. Nevertheless, the question remains, in what sense may religious freedom be called a "Christian" principle? The Council answers by saying that the principle has its "roots in divine revelation." These roots are explored in the second part of the Declaration. This section is of high ecumenical significance. It will furnish a major theme of ecumenical dialogue.

25. Cf. CIC, c. 1351; Pius XII, allocution to prelate auditors and other officials and administrators of the tribune of the Holy Roman Rota, Oct. 6, 1946: AAS 38 (1946), p. 394; idem, encyclical "Mystici Corporis," June 29, 1943: AAS (1943), p. 243.

26. The unwavering Christian dogma that the act of Christian faith must be a free response to the Word and grace of God reveals the divine respect for human freedom and for man's inalienable responsibility toward the direction of his own life. The constitutional principle of religious freedom is not a conclusion from this Christian dogma. The connection is rather more historical. That is to say, given the Christian doctrine of the freedom of faith, men would gradually come—as over the centuries they have come—to realize that man's religious life is an affair of responsible freedom, from which all coercion is to be excluded. Given this Christian appreciation of the value of freedom (and given also the growing secular experience of freedom as a social value and a political end), men could not fail to become increasingly conscious that religious freedom is an exigency of the dignity of the person, as this dignity is disclosed by the revelation that man is made in the image of God. Moreover, experience would also make it clear that, where religious freedom prevails, a climate of freedom is created in society which itself favors the free preaching of the gospel and the free living of the Christian life.

27. Cf. Lactantius "Divinarum Institutionum," Book V. 19: CSEL 19, pp. 463-464, 465: PL 6, 614 and 616 (ch. 20); St. Ambrose, "Epistola ad Valentianum Imp.," Letter 21: PL 16, 1005; St. Augustine,

The act of faith is of its very nature a free act. Man, redeemed by Christ the Savior and through Christ Jesus called to be God's adopted son,[28] cannot give his adherence to God revealing Himself unless the Father draw him [29] to offer to God the reasonable and free submission of faith.

It is therefore completely in accord with the nature of faith that in matters religious every manner of coercion on the part of men should be excluded. In consequence, the principle of religious freedom makes no small contribution to the creation of an environment in which men can without hindrance be invited to Christian faith, and embrace it of their own free will, and profess it effectively in their whole manner of life.

11. God calls men to serve Him in spirit and in truth. Hence they are bound in conscience but they stand under no compulsion.[30] God has regard for the dignity of the human person

---

"Contra Litteras Petiliani," Book II, ch. 83: CSEL 52, p. 112: PL 43, 315; cf. C. 23, q. 5, c. 33 (ed. Friedberg, col. 939); idem, Letter 23: PL 33, 98; idem, Letter 34: PL 33, 132; idem, Letter 35: PL 33, 135; St. Gregory the Great, "Epistola ad Virgilium et Theodorum Episcopos Massiliae Galliarum," Register of Letters I, 45: MGH Ep. 1, p. 72; PL 77, 510-511 (Book I, ep. 47); idem, "Epistola ad Johannem Episcopum Constantinopolitanum," Register of Letters, III, 52: MGH Letter 1, p. 210: PL 77, 649 (Book III, Letter 53); cf. D. 45, c. 1 (ed. Friedberg, col. 160); Council of Toledo IV, c. 57: Mansi 10, 633; cf. D. 45, c. 5 (ed. Friedberg, col. 161-162); Clement III: X., V. 6, 9: ed. Friedberg, col. 774; Innocent III, "Epistola ad Arelatensem Archiepiscopum," X., III, 42, 3: ed. Friedberg, col. 646.

28. Cf. *Eph. 1:5.*
29. Cf. *Jn. 6:44.*
30. The major purpose here is to show, from the example and teaching of Christ Himself, that coercion in matters religious is alien to the spirit of the gospel. The ways of God with men are not coercive. They are the ways of faithful love. And their supreme illustration is the cross. Rather than impose the truth upon men by force, Christ willingly accepted death at their hands, and He made His death itself the means of redemption, as the revelation of a love than which there is no greater. The way of Christ became the way of His first apostles, whose reliance was on the power of the Word of God, never on earthly forces.

whom He Himself created; man is to be guided by his own judgment and he is to enjoy freedom.

This truth appears at its height in Christ Jesus, in whom God perfectly manifested Himself and His ways with men. Christ is our Master and our Lord.[31] He is also meek and humble of heart.[32] And in attracting and inviting His disciples He acted patiently.[33] He wrought miracles to shed light on His teaching and to establish its truth. But His intention was to rouse faith in His bearers and to confirm them in faith, not to exert coercion upon them.[34]

He did indeed denounce the unbelief of some who listened to Him; but He left vengeance to God in expectation of the day of judgment.[35] When He sent His apostles into the world, He said to them: "He who believes and is baptized shall be saved, but he who does not believe shall be condemned" (Mk. 16:16); but He Himself, noting that cockle had been sown amid the wheat, gave orders that both should be allowed to grow until the harvest time, which will come at the end of the world.[36]

He refused to be a political Messiah, ruling by force;[37] He preferred to call Himself the Son of Man, who came "to serve and to give his life as a ransom for many" (Mk. 10:45). He showed Himself the perfect Servant of God;[38] "a bruised reed he will not break, and a smoking wick he will not quench" (Mt. 12:20).

He acknowledged the power of government and its rights, when He commanded that tribute be given to Caesar. But He gave clear warning that the higher rights of God are to be kept inviolate: "Render, therefore, to Caesar the things that

31. Cf. Jn. 13:13.
32. Cf. Mt. 11:29.
33. Cf. Mt. 11:28-30; Jn. 6:67-68.
34. Cf. Mt. 9:28-29; Mk. 9:23-24; 6, 5-6; Paul VI, encyclical "Ecclesiam Suam," Aug. 6, 1964: AAS 56 (1964), pp. 642-643.
35. Cf. Mt. 11:20-24; Rom. 12:19-20; 2 Th. 1:8.
36. Cf. Mt. 13:30 and 40-42.
37. Cf. Mt. 4:8-10; Jn. 6:15.
38. Cf. Is. 42:1-4.

are Caesar's, and to God the things that are God's" (Mt. 22:21).

In the end, when He completed on the cross the work of redemption whereby He achieved salvation and true freedom for men, He also brought His revelation to completion. He bore witness to the truth,[39] but He refused to impose the truth by force on those who spoke against it. Not by force of blows does His rule assert its claims.[40] Rather, it is established by witnessing to the truth and by hearing the truth, and it extends its dominion by the love whereby Christ, lifted up on the cross, draws all men to Himself.[41]

Taught by the word and example of Christ, the apostles followed the same way. From the very origins of the Church the disciples of Christ strove to convert men to faith in Christ as the Lord—not, however, by the use of coercion or by devices unworthy of the gospel, but by the power, above all, of the Word of God.[42] Steadfastly they proclaimed to all the plan of God our Savior, "who wishes all men to be saved and to come to the knowledge of the truth" (I Tim. 2:4). At the same time, however, they showed respect for weaker souls even though these persons were in error. Thus they made it plain that "every one of us will render an account of himself to God" (Rom. 14:12),[43] and for this reason is bound to obey his conscience.

Like Christ Himself, the apostles were unceasingly bent upon bearing witness to the truth of God. They showed special courage in speaking "the word of God with boldness" (Acts 4:31) [44] before the people and their rulers. With a firm faith they held that the gospel is indeed the power of God unto salvation for all who believe.[45] Therefore they rejected all

---

39. Cf. *Jn. 18:37.*
40. Cf. *Mt. 26:51-53; Jn. 18:36.*
41. Cf. *Jn. 12:32.*
42. Cf. *1 Cor. 2:3-5; 1 Th. 2:3-5.*
43. Cf. *Rom. 14:1-23; 1 Cor. 8:9-13; 10:23-33.*
44. Cf. *Eph. 6:19-20.*
45. Cf. *Rom. 1:16.*

"carnal weapons." [46] They followed the example of the gentleness and respectfulness of Christ. And they preached the Word of God in the full confidence that there was resident in this Word itself a divine power able to destroy all the forces arrayed against God [47] and to bring men to faith in Christ and to His service.[48] As the Master, so too the apostles recognized legitimate civil authority. "For there exists no authority except from God," the Apostle teaches, and therefore commands: * "Let everyone be subject to the higher authorities . . . : he who resists the authority resists the ordinance of God" (Rom. 13:1-2).[49]

At the same time, however, they did not hesitate to speak out against governing powers which set themselves in opposition to the holy will of God: "We must obey God rather than men" (Acts 5:29).[50] This is the way along which countless martyrs and other believers have walked through all ages and over all the earth.

12. The Church therefore is being faithful to the truth of the gospel, and is following the way of Christ and the apostles when she recognizes, and gives support to, the principle of religious freedom as befitting the dignity of man and as being in accord with divine revelation. Throughout the ages, the Church has kept safe and handed on the doctrine received from the Master and from the apostles. In the life of the People of God as it has made its pilgrim way through the vicissitudes of human history, there have at times appeared ways of acting which were less in accord with the spirit of the gospel and even opposed to it.[51] Nevertheless, the doctrine

---

46. Cf. 2 Cor. 10:4; 1 Th. 5:8-9.
47. Cf. Eph. 6:11-17.
48. Cf. 2 Cor. 10:3-5.
* The preceding 14 words are missing from the L'Osservatore Romano text of Dec. 11, 1965.—Ed.
49. Cf. 1 Pet. 2:13-17.
50. Cf. Acts 4:19-20.
51. The historical consciousness of the Council required that it be loyal to the truth of history. Hence the Declaration makes the humble avowal that the People of God have not always walked in the way of Christ and the apostles. At times they have followed ways

of the Church that no one is to be coerced into faith has always stood firm.

Thus the leaven of the gospel has long been about its quiet work in the minds of men. To it is due in great measure the fact that in the course of time men have come more widely to recognize their dignity as persons, and the conviction has grown stronger that in religious matters the person in society is to be kept free from all manner of human coercion.

13. Among the things which concern the good of the Church and indeed the welfare of society here on earth—things therefore which are always and everywhere to be kept secure and defended against all injury—this certainly is preeminent, namely, that the Church should enjoy that full measure of freedom which her care for the salvation of men requires.[52] This freedom is sacred, because the only-begotten Son endowed with it the Church which He purchased with His blood. It is so much the property of the Church that to act against it is to act against the will of God. The freedom of the Church is the fundamental principle in what concerns the relations between the Church and governments and the whole civil order.[53]

---

that were at variance with the spirit of the gospel and even contrary to it. The avowal is made briefly and without details. But the intention was to confess, in a penitent spirit, not only that Christian churchmen and princes have appealed to the coercive instruments of power in the supposed interests of the faith, but also that the Church herself has countenanced institutions which made a similar appeal. Whatever may be the nice historical judgment on these institutions in their own context of history, they are not to be justified, much less are they ever or in any way to be reinstated. The Declaration is a final renouncement and repudiation by the Church of all means and measures of coercion in matters religious.

52. Cf. *Leo XIII, letter "Officio Sanctissimo," Dec. 22, 1887: AAS 20 (1887), p. 269; idem letter "Ex Litteris," Apr. 7, 1887: AAS 19 (1886), p. 465.*

53. This statement, together with the declaration of religious freedom as a human right and the enunciation of the principle of the free society, must rank as one of the central doctrinal utterances of

In human society and in the face of government, the Church claims freedom for herself in her character as a spiritual authority, established by Christ the Lord. Upon this authority there rests, by divine mandate, the duty of going out into the whole world and preaching the gospel to every creature.[54] The Church also claims freedom for herself in her character as a society of men who have the right to live in society in accordance with the precepts of Christian faith.[55]

In turn, where the principle of religious freedom is not only proclaimed in words or simply incorporated in law but also given sincere and practical application, there the Church succeeds in achieving a stable situation of right as well as of fact and the independence which is necessary for the fulfillment of her divine mission. This independence is precisely what the authorities of the Church claim in society.[56]

At the same time, the Christian faithful, in common with all other men, possess the civil right not to be hindered in leading their lives in accordance with their conscience. There-

---

the Declaration. Its importance is emphasized by the fact that Paul VI quoted it in his address on Dec. 9 to political rulers: "And what is it that this Church asks of you, after nearly two thousand years of all sorts of vicissitudes in her relations with you, the powers of earth? What does the Church ask of you today? In one of the major texts of the Council she has told you: she asks of you nothing but freedom—the freedom to believe and to preach her faith, the freedom to love God and to serve Him, the freedom to live and to bring to men her message of life." This doctrine is traditional; it is also new. Implicit in it is the renunciation by the Church of a condition of legal privilege in society. The Church does not make, as a matter of right or of divine law, the claim that she should be established as the "religion of the state." Her claim is freedom, nothing more.

54. Cf. *Mk. 16:15; Mt. 28:18-20;* Pius XII, encyclical *"Summi Pontificatus,"* Oct. 20, 1939: *AAS* 31 (1939), pp. 445-446.
55. Cf. Pius XI, letter *"Firmissimam Constantiam,"* Mar. 28, 1937: *AAS* 29 (1937), p. 196.
56. Cf. Pius XII, allocution *"Ci Riesce,"* Dec. 6, 1953: *AAS* 45 (1953), p. 802.

fore, a harmony exists between the freedom of the Church and the religious freedom which is to be recognized as the right of all men and communities and sanctioned by constitutional law.

14. In order to be faithful to the divine command, "Make disciples of all nations" (Mt. 28:19), the Catholic Church must work with all urgency and concern "that the Word of God * may run and be glorified" (2 Th. 3:1). Hence the Church earnestly begs of her children that, first of all, "supplications, prayers, intercessions, and thanksgivings be made for all men. . . . For this is good and agreeable in the sight of God our Savior, who wishes all men to be saved and to come to the knowledge of the truth" (1 Tim. 2:1-4).

In the formation of their consciences, the Christian faithful ought carefully to attend to the sacred and certain doctrine of the Church.[57,58] The Church is, by the will of Christ, the teacher of the truth. It is her duty to give utterance to, and authoritatively to teach, that Truth which is Christ Himself, and also to declare and confirm by her authority those principles of the moral order which have their origin in human nature itself. Furthermore, let Christians walk in wisdom in the face of those outside, "in the Holy Spirit, in unaffected love, in the word of truth" (2 Cor. 6:6-7). Let them be about

---

* The CCD translation has "the Lord" instead of "God."—Ed.

57. Cf. *Pius XII, radio message, Mar 23, 1952: AAS 44 (1952), pp. 270-278.*

58. The Council directs a word of pastoral exhortation to the Christian faithful. They are urged, in particular, to form their consciences under the guidance of the authority of the Church. It might be noted here that the Council intended to make a clear distinction between religious freedom as a principle in the civil order and the Christian freedom which obtains even inside the Church. These two freedoms are distinct in kind; and it would be perilous to confuse them. Nowhere does the Declaration touch the issue of freedom within the Church. Undoubtedly, however, it will be a stimulus for the articulation of a full theology of Christian freedom in its relation to the doctrinal and disciplinary authority of the Church.

their task of spreading the light of life with all confidence [59] and apostolic courage, even to the shedding of their blood.

The disciple is bound by a grave obligation toward Christ his Master ever more adequately to understand the truth received from Him, faithfully to proclaim it, and vigorously to defend it, never—be it understood—having recourse to means that are incompatible with the spirit of the gospel. At the same time, the charity of Christ urges him to act lovingly, prudently and patiently in his dealings with those who are in error or in ignorance with regard to the faith.[60] All is to be taken into account—the Christian duty to Christ, the life-giving Word which must be proclaimed, the rights of the human person, and the measure of grace granted by God through Christ to men, who are invited freely to accept and profess the faith.

15. The fact is that men of the present day want to be able freely to profess their religion in private and in public. Religious freedom has already been declared to be a civil right in most constitutions, and it is solemnly recognized in international documents.[61] The further fact is that forms of government still exist under which, even though freedom of religious worship receives constitutional recognition, the powers of government are engaged in the effort to deter citizens from the profession of religion and to make life difficult and dangerous for religious Communities.[62]

59. Cf. *Acts 4:29.*
60. Cf. *John XXIII,* encyclical *"Pacem in Terris," Apr. 11, 1963: AAS 55 (1963), pp. 299-300.*
61. Cf. *John XXIII,* encyclical *"Pacem in Terris," Apr. 11, 1963: AAS 55 (1963), pp. 295-296.*
62. At the end, the Council turns once more to the world at large. Two facts claim its attention. First, the principle of religious freedom is widely recognized; this fact takes its place among the signs of the times. Second, the principle of religious freedom is also widely violated; this fact can only be deplored. Then the Declaration, which has stated its argument in terms of principle, turns to the pragmatic aspect of the issue—the practical value and necessity of religious freedom in the world today. It is a world of diversity which is striving toward some measure of unity; it is a world of conflict which is yearning for peace; it is, above all, a world in

This sacred Synod greets with joy the first of these two facts, as among the signs of the times. With sorrow, however, it denounces the other fact, as only to be deplored. The Synod exhorts Catholics, and it directs a plea to all men, most carefully to consider how greatly necessary religious freedom is, especially in the present condition of the human family.

All nations are coming into even closer unity. Men of different cultures and religions are being brought together in closer relationships. There is a growing consciousness of the personal responsibility that weighs upon every man. All this is evident.

Consequently, in order that relationships of peace and harmony may be established and maintained within the whole of mankind, it is necessary that religious freedom be everywhere provided with an effective constitutional guarantee, and that respect be shown for the high duty and right of man freely to lead his religious life in society.

May the God and Father of all grant that the human family, through careful observance of the principle of religious freedom in society, may be brought by the grace of Christ and the power of the Holy Spirit to the sublime and unending "freedom of the glory of the sons of God" (Rom. 8:21).

Each and every one of the things set forth in this Declaration has won the consent of the Fathers of this most sacred Council. We too, by the apostolic authority conferred on us by Christ, join with the Venerable Fathers in approving, decreeing, and establishing these things in the Holy Spirit, and we direct that what has thus been enacted in synod be published to God's glory.

Rome, at St. Peter's, December 7, 1965

I, Paul, Bishop of the Catholic Church

There follow the signatures of the Fathers.

---

which a new consciousness of human dignity struggles to find expression in social institutions that will guarantee to men the freedom which is due to them in justice. Most necessary of all is freedom of religion. Where it is safe, the way is open for the "glorious freedom of the sons of God" to come to men as God's gift through Christ in the Holy Spirit.

Notes on Contributors

JOHN COURTNEY MURRAY, S.J., is one of the outstanding names in Catholic theology today and is an expert on the problem of church-state relations. He served as a *peritus* to Vatican Council II and was instrumental in drafting the document, Declaration on Religious Freedom. He received his doctorate in sacred theology from the Gregorian University in Rome and has been professor of sacred theology at Woodstock College since 1937. Father Murray served as the first editor of *Theological Studies*, was a member of the Advisory Committee to the Secretary of Defense (1962), and is associated with the Center for the Study of Democratic Institutions. Among his published books are: *We Hold These Truths* and *The Problem of God*.

JERALD C. BRAUER received a Ph.D. from the University of Chicago in 1948. Having begun his teaching career with the University of Chicago as an assistant professor of church history, he has been dean of the University of Chicago Divinity School since 1960. In 1961 he was visiting professor at the University of Frankfurt in Germany. His reputation as a theologian easily qualified him to be an observer at Vatican Council II. His books include: *Protestantism in America*, *Basic Questions for the Christian Scholar*, and *Luther and the Reformation*.

FRANCIS J. CANAVAN, S.J., has been an associate editor of *America* magazine since 1960. He received his Ph.D. in political science from Duke University in 1957. He is the author of many articles in numerous periodicals and has written *The Political Reason of Edmund Burke.*

VICTOR G. ROSENBLUM, member of the faculty of Northwestern University since 1957, received his Ph.D. in political science in 1953 from the University of California at Berkeley. He has been editor-in-chief of *Administrative Law Review,* and cochairman of the Joint Committee on Political Science and Administrative Law of the American Political Science Association and the Association of American Law Schools. He is the author of *Law as a Political Instrument* and coauthor of *The Uses of Power.*

JOHN L. McKENZIE, S.J., is one of the outstanding Biblical scholars of the Catholic Church in the United States. He was professor of Sacred Scripture for eighteen years at West Baden College, the Jesuit seminary formerly located in southern Indiana. His many books include *The Two-Edged Sword, Myths and Realities, The Power and the Wisdom, The World of the Judges,* and the crown of many years of meticulously accumulated scholarship, his monumental *Dictionary of the Bible.* Father McKenzie was professor of Biblical history at Loyola University, Chicago, and in 1965 accepted the invitation of visiting professor of the Divinity School of the University of Chicago. He is immediate past president of the Catholic Biblical Association and current president of the Society for Biblical Literature.

PHILIP S. DENENFELD is a staff associate of the American Association of University Professors (AAUP). His duties include handling complaints alleging violations of academic freedom and tenure, and giving staff service to the two national committees on professional ethics and on problems of academic freedom in Church-related institutions. He has spoken and written on such topics as theory and practice in the area of First Amendment rights, with emphasis on problems of censorship and church-state relations. Dr. Denenfeld holds a

Ph.D. from Northwestern University (1957) and currently is professor of English on leave from Western Michigan University.

J. V. LANGMEAD CASSERLEY received his doctorate of literature from the University of London and thereupon lectured at University College of the South-West, Exeter. He took residence in the United States to become Mary Crooke Hoffman Professor of Dogmatic Theology at the General Theological Seminary in New York, and subsequently and currently is professor of apologetics at Seabury-Western Theological Seminary in Evanston, Illinois. His many books include: *The Fate of Modern Culture, No Faith My Own, The Christian in Philosophy*, and *Crucified Reason, the Contribution of Reason to Theology*.

DAVID NOEL FREEDMAN is one of the outstanding Protestant Biblical scholars in the world today. He received his Ph.D. in Semitic languages, history, and archaeology from Johns Hopkins University in 1948. He has since published numerous articles in both journals and books, has served a term as editor of *The Journal of Biblical Literature*, and has begun collaboration as coeditor with his former teacher, Professor Wm. Foxwell Albright, on the significant Anchor Bible Series. In 1964 he accepted a position at San Fransciso Theological Seminary, where he is professor of Old Testament and, simultaneously, professor of the same at the Graduate Theological Union.

GEORGE G. V. M. VAN MASSENHOVE, S.J., attended Vatican Council II as a *peritus* to a group of bishops of northern India. His linguistic skill and theological background qualified him for this important post. Having received his degree in Theology from Louvain in 1950, Father Van Massenhove taught theology at Notre Dame College, Antwerp. His background in ecumenical work freed him from teaching in order to lecture on subjects in the field of ecumenism. He is at present guest lecturer at the Bellarmine School of Theology, North Aurora, Illinois.